# MONIQUE MEAK'S CASE

BRIAN CADWALLADER © 2018
briancad@yahoo.com

Dedicated to my Third Grade teacher

Mrs. Fern Carroll McDaniel

Who showed me the way.


Many thanks to the readers

whose comments made this revision

a better book.

# CHAPTER 1

Thanks to a 14-year-old mama who wouldn't give up her quarts of beer and crack cocaine, Monique Meak was born prematurely and with fetal alcohol syndrome in July 1991. The baby was small in size and microencephalic, meaning her brain and skull were strikingly smaller than the doctor's fist. The hospital kept her for weeks in the NICU. She received surgery to fix a heart defect. The hospital weaned her from the drugs and waited to see if she would learn to breathe on her own despite her severe asthma.

In the meantime, her mama, Lana Meak, was arrested at the hospital and charged with child endangerment. But, after just two weeks she was released from jail because the District Attorney refused to prosecute her. Microencephaly is not exclusively a product of fetal exposure to alcohol and drugs. It can also be caused by disease or genetics. This meant Lana would probably not have been convicted. There was reasonable doubt about exactly what caused Monique's brain damage.

Lana took Monique home from the hospital to the home of her mother, Rose Meak. Monique's father, Demetrius Jackson, was age 19 and lived with his own mother, Sarah Thompson. Both families welcomed and fussed over the new baby. She would be raised by Lana and Rose, and sometimes Demetrius and Sarah would help out.

Monique hardly thrived and she was slow to develop. Early on she cried much of the time. Lana was told it was colic but no matter what she or Rose did Monique could not be soothed. She did not grow normally or gain weight. After months went by, Monique finally began sleeping at night, but she did not recognize faces, reward attention, smile or show love. By six months her eyes did not track together; rather, one or the other would roll outwards, giving her a google-eyed look.

The constant burden of caring for the unrewarding Monique took a toll on teenaged Lana and grandmother Rose. Lana did not like being chained to her daughter. She resented having to care for the child all the time. For these reasons Lana became depressed and starting drinking and doing coke again. Lana began to find excuses to leave Monique with Rose so she could get out of the house and find a life of her own. Lana got a cashier's job at a Burger King. Demetrius was soon out of the picture, having fallen in with a street gang and getting arrested for armed robbery. Pretty much Monique was Rose's baby to raise, with a little help from the other grandmother Sarah.

Monique did not learn to roll over and crawl until after the age of two years, nor did she learn to use any words that could be understood. Her balance and coordination were iffy. It took a very long time before she learned to pull herself up and toddle. She had no control over her impulses, and often injured herself by bumping into things, or falling or throwing herself to the ground. She did this several times per day. She did the same thing again and again, not learning from her experience. She was covered with bruises. It became plain that something was not right about Monique. Her brain damage made her irreversibly mentally retarded and hyperactive. She was still in diapers at three years.

Somebody, probably grandmother Sarah, called Child Protection and told them that Lana and Rose were neglecting Monique by not caring for her properly, and were abusing her by beating her for failing to listen. The OCS social workers went to Rose's house and found it strewn with garbage ankle-deep. Nothing had been thrown out for months. There was a strong odor of dirty diapers and cat urine and feces coming from the garbage. A couple dead cats were found, and another dozen or so emaciated cats wandered about. The social workers had Lana and Rose fetch Monique. She was found in a soiled T-shirt and dirty diaper. Her head and body were covered in bruises. She was thin with a bloated belly and just barely surviving. When asked how the baby got the marks, Lana said she fell or knocked herself against the furniture. The social workers took Monique away and put her in a foster home.

To get a hold order from the Juvenile Court, the social workers prepared an affidavit in August 1995. In the affidavit, the social workers stated that Lana Meak had a history with OCS of several valid cases for abuse and neglect and had not straightened out despite receiving services from the Family Services Unit. The same affidavit complained that there was no food in the house, and Monique Meak seemed to have lost some weight since last seen by OCS. The affidavit said the New Orleans Police Department arrested Lana Meak for intentional non-support of her child.

A December 1995 psychotherapy evaluation concluded that Lana Meak was a troubled young woman.

Lana's version of most all significant details of her life is markedly different from what has been reported. Clearly, she assumes no responsibility for her actions and, instead, blames others. There is nothing that would suggest any psychotic functioning, but her judgment and reasoning abilities are faulty and she has no insight into her behaviors. Lana is emotionally immature and seems to have had very little positive experiences in either receiving or delivering adequate parenting. She very definitely needs parenting classes to help her understand the needs of her child and she should continue in her independent living program. However, she is resistant and sees little use for such intervention. Despite her denials, continued participation in a substance abuse program also seems warranted. Even at this relative young age, Lana seems to already be displaying many characteristics of a Personality Disorder and seems to have had major difficulties in various areas of her life. Any additional interventions however, will only serve to lower the level of compliance as it seems highly likely that Lana will simply "do nothing." In any event, much improvements in stability should be demonstrated prior to attempts at reunification.

The December 1995 OCS court letter recounted that Monique was found hungry, dirty, her hair uncombed and matted, her legs marked with sores, and she smelled of urine. At that time Lana Meak was incarcerated in Orleans Parish Prison.

Among other orders meant to reunite mother and daughter, the Juvenile Court told Lana Meak to comply with court-ordered visitation. Lana did not do this. The Taco Bell job she accepted in July 1996 conflicted with the visitation schedule. A year later OCS reported that Lana did not regularly visit Monique despite the foster parent's willingness to accommodate the visit. Nor did Lana comply with the court ordered substance abuse counseling and monitoring. She quit both the BASIC and NOSAC programs after just a few sessions.

Monique reached age 4 apart from her mother. Lana did not get her daughter back because she was still using drugs and didn't have an appropriate place to live. Baby daddy Demetrius was still in prison. Monique was on her third set of foster parents. The earlier ones gave Monique back to the state because she required too much constant care. That's why the social workers chose Barbara and Charles White.

The Whites lived in a modest two story ranch-style brick house in an older subdivision of New Orleans East. The homes there were originally built for the white flight from the City during the civil rights turmoil in the 1960's but, over the next twenty years or so, most of them were re-sold to working class black families. The Whites moved in not long after they were married, and had lived there seven years. They had two sons, Charles Jr. age six and Aaron age five. Aaron was adopted. Because of severe pre-eclampsia, Barbara's tubes were tied and she would bear no more children. Barbara was a stay-at-home mother. Charles White drove a city bus. He left for work at 4 a.m. and returned home around 2 p.m. Their home was asleep every day by 8 p.m.

The Whites first became curious about being foster parents when they heard the financial benefits were good. A second income would be great, and Barbara would not have to leave home to earn it. A regular foster child came with a tax-free stipend of $850 per month, plus food stamps and free medical insurance, and with a beneficial income tax deduction. So the Whites tried it a few years and they did just fine. When they learned that more money was paid for children who needed extra attention, the Whites agreed to try. After a few training classes and a home inspection, the Whites were certified as therapeutic foster parents and were given Monique.

She turned the White household upside down. From the moment she awoke until she fell asleep at night, Monique was hyperactive and needed constant supervision. The Whites could not take their eyes off the child for even a few moments lest she hurt herself or get into something and destroy it. She repeatedly pulled down curtains and knocked to the floor anything resting on a table. She opened doors and emptied cupboards until the Whites installed child-proof hardware. She threw toys and beat on the dog. She ate out of the garbage can. She could not be taken anywhere without launching into repeated tantrums. Monique did these things again and again no matter the amount of warning or correction. The child would not learn. She had no appreciation for her conduct, no sense of right or wrong or action and consequences. Once she swung a broom around and dented the family's big screen TV. Most disconcerting was Monique's chronic diarrhea. She had six or seven stools per day. And she had a nasty habit of peeling off her diaper and smearing the contents on the walls, furniture, dog and floor. To keep the diapers on her the Whites would wrap them with duct tape.

After only three months Monique was removed from the Whites' home because she was scalded in the bathtub. It happened on the afternoon of Super Bowl Sunday. According to the Whites, Charles and the boys were downstairs in the den preparing the new wide-screen television for the game. Barbara was downstairs in the kitchen. Suddenly Monique let loose with a loud, high pitched scream from upstairs. She could be heard in every corner of the house. Somehow she had gotten away from them. Somehow she had removed her diaper, put the stopper in the tub drain, turned on the hot water faucet, and then climbed in. Charles and Barbara ran to her and pulled the wailing child from the bathtub. They wrapped her in a sheet and, deciding not to wait for an ambulance, drove her for a half hour across town to Children's Hospital. Monique could not be consoled; she sobbed all the way to the hospital.

# CHAPTER 2

Monique Meak presented at the Children's Hospital ER at almost sundown on Super Bowl Sunday. She was wrapped in a damp sheet and sobbing. She was accompanied by the entire White family.

Medical examination revealed Monique to be a small black female, approximately age four. She was alert and in pain from a large scald to her posterior, her vagina, and the back of her legs. The right leg had deep second degree burns. About 10% of her tiny body was scalded. Her head, body, arms, hands and feet were not burned. There were no splash burns. The uniformity of the backside burns, and no extremity burns, indicated that Monique had been placed into the bathtub. To the ER doctor, all this was suspicious for the child being forced to sit in very hot water, her hands and feet held out of it. The doctor decided the scald had not been caused by self-injury. He felt someone put her in the hot water, but he could not determine intent. Perhaps it was to clean a soiled child, or perhaps it was deliberately meant to cause pain. Pain-killing burn salve and bandages were applied and Monique was admitted to the hospital.

Then, the ER doctor confronted the Whites with his suspicion that someone had scalded Monique. They denied any involvement. The doctor reported the injury to the State social workers who told the Whites that Monique would not be going home with them. The social workers decided that even if no one from the White family had immersed Monique into the hot water, then at the least the Whites had failed to keep the child under supervision. The social workers reported the incident to the judge and attorneys involved in Monique's foster care case. One of those attorneys was Thomas Frazier, child's counsel.

# CHAPTER 3

Frazier went to the hospital to visit his client. He found Monique asleep in a large crib, curled on her side and facing the wall. She was swathed in bandages from her lower back to her feet. The nurse said Monique was comfortable and recovering well. She said Monique was almost uncontrollable when awake, and had to constantly be supervised lest she climb out of the crib and injure herself.

Next, Frazier reviewed Monique's chart. He found the report by the ER doctor saying the injury was probably not self-inflicted. The doctor had also made a sketch of the scald pattern showing the burn to the lower half of Monique's body. Frazier asked to speak to the doctor, but he was away from the hospital. Frazier obtained a copy of the chart and left.

The chart revealed the torture Monique suffered at the hospital. First they gave her powerful pain drugs. Next, she was wheeled into the tub room and put into water. She had to soak because the fluids oozing from Monique's wounds stuck to her bandages. Once the bandages were removed the debridement began. This means the naked girl was put on her belly and stretched across a table. A TV was put down low where she could see a children's show like Sesame Street. Then the nurses grabbed her and held her down so she can't move. Then they reached for a bristly brush and scrubbed, scrubbed, scrubbed the dead skin away. The better the scrubbing, the better the healing. But TV and drugs did not stop Monique from feeling more pain. She would scream and scream, not understanding that the nurses were trying to help. When the nurses finished scrubbing they put fresh bandages on Monique and moved her back to her room. This routine was repeated every day for almost three weeks.

Next, Frazier got a copy of the social worker records. They showed that the Whites home was actually a Therapeutic Foster Care home, a sort of super-foster care home which was supposed to provide constant supervision appropriate for a hyperactive, retarded four-year-old. The social worker records did not shed more light on how the scalding happened except for one thing: Monique told a social worker that Mr. Charlie put her in the bathtub.

# CHAPTER 4

Frazier decided that Monique had been scalded either intentionally or through neglect. Even if she did it to herself, she was too young to be blamed for it. Her injuries were severe and might leave lasting physical and mental scars. Foster care was supposed to salvage Monique, but it ruined her.

Because he was Monique's Juvenile Court lawyer it was up to him and no one else to do something about it. If Frazier did not timely sue those responsible, or find someone else to take the case, then Monique could turn around any time before age 19 and sue Frazier for legal malpractice.

Frazier knew how to sue for personal injuries. After passing the bar he clerked for five years with the city's premier plaintiff's firm. There he learned how to handle cases for people injured in car accidents. He did all the back office work except actually trying the few cases that went to trial. In order to get courtroom experience Frazier began volunteering at juvenile court as child's counsel in abuse and neglect cases.

Frazier had one foot in the civil world and one in the juvenile. When he left that firm Frazier started his own personal injury law firm. For the next six years he worked alone, at home, without any help from a secretary or a clerk. It was not unusual for Frazier to go to a hearing at court, or a meeting at another attorney's office, and then return to his home office and work for hours at the computer. It was not unusual for Frazier to work long hours every day, weekends included, for more than 80 hours per week. By this effort he provided a modest living for his family, and he hoped to grow his firm.

There was never a regular cash flow. Frazier only had money when the cases settled, and he barely had enough cases to keep the bills and credit cards paid. It helped a lot that his wife worked as a clerk in a hospital which gave them a steady basic income and medical insurance. They drove two older cars handed down by his mother-in-law, and they had a modest mortgage on a house that desperately needed painting. Their only extravagance was Catholic school tuition for their three daughters.

All Frazier ever wanted was to solve cases for people less fortunate than he. In 11 years of practice Frazier learned plenty about juvenile court, and about civil motions and bench trials and appeals, but he had never tried a jury trial. Easily 99% of civil cases settled before trial. If this were not so the courts would be clogged. Actually, true jury trial lawyers were a rare breed. And Monique's case had all the hallmarks of a good jury case – a sympathetic plaintiff, tremendous injury, deep pocket defendants, and a generous jury pool.

Frazier feared failing as a trial lawyer -- not for lack of intelligence, and not for lack of preparation. It was because Frazier had a mental illness, manic depression or bipolar 1. It dogged him for half his life.

Twenty years had passed since he first suffered a psychotic break, and 11 years had passed since his last hospitalization. Frazier knew a lot about managing the disease in stressful times. He learned to be vigilant to keep the mania in check. He knew how to medicate it. He was confident the disease was controlled at least most of the time. However, in the back of his mind, he feared the wreck unchained mania caused and he worried it would surface in the middle of trial. His performance at Monique's trial would be a major test of the manic curse. It would tell whether he had the right stuff or not.

There was no neutrality for Frazier. He could not help getting emotionally involved in his client's case. For this reason, he constantly second-guessed his emotions. Was he dispassionate enough, or was he distracted by being too close? He learned how to harness the mania, working into the high swings while avoiding anything consequential during the low periods.

Frazier was not a handsome man. He was overweight, and had a hare lip and glasses. Classmates used to call him "four eyes and squiggly lip." He had a scar revision to the lip at age 17, but it didn't go as well as hoped. His anger and disappointment were tremendous. Frazier very seldom dated. At socials, he tended to stand at the outside. He feared powerful women. In spite of this introversion, Frazier knew that he was going to have to let the jury "see" the real person who represented the helpless child, and that prospect made him nervous. While in his head Frazier savored the chance to talk about the emotional pain of being ugly, in his heart he was afraid. It's hard enough being fully vulnerable with just one person. At trial there will be 12 strangers in the jury box, plus the judge and six lawyers hanging on to his every word.

Frazier struggled with how to translate the jury's natural loathing of visibly ugly into understanding the mind-fuck that being ugly does. He identified with Monique's disfigurement and the emotional turmoil of a damaged self-image. How lucky that Frazier was gifted enough to fend for himself. How lucky that he was able to champion those less fortunate than he. People like Monique are not disposable. She is no less worthy than anyone else, though she be female, young, black, poor, retarded, unloved, neglected, and abused.

Frazier thirsted for a big win. Financially, her case would be a big deal. His earnings would hugely valuate his quality as a lawyer. In the short run, litigating Monique's case would mean a good deal more debt, but Frazier had always juggled debt. He would tap his credit cards to invest in the necessary expenses of the case. Emotionally and financially he knew he could sustain the pre-trial litigation. He would just have to be very careful with the mania when the stressful jury trial began.

Frazier felt this was his moment. He felt the risks had to be taken.

# CHAPTER 5

Frazier asked the Juvenile Court to appoint tutors to review the matter. The judge named attorneys Alberta Jones and Michael Harmon as tutrix and undertutor. Frazier met with them and they approved a suit for damages, and approved his contract for a one-third contingency attorney's fee and expenses.

To draft the suit, Frazier needed service addresses for each of the defendants. He asked the social workers for the Whites' address but was refused on privacy grounds. So Frazier hired a private detective who quickly uncovered it.

Frazier then prepared this suit:

## PETITION

The petition of M.M., by her undersigned counsel, respectfully represents:

1.

M.M. is a minor domiciled in Orleans Parish and is adjudicated as a child in need of care within the legal custody of the Department of Social Services.

2.

Acting for M.M. is her provisional dative tutrix ad litem, Alberta Jones, Esq., duly appointed by the Orleans Parish Juvenile Court.

3.

Made defendants are:

A. Barbara White, wife of/and Charles White, adult residents of Orleans Parish.

B. ABC Insurance Co. is the insurer providing homeowner's liability and/or medical payments coverage to Barbara White, wife of/and Charles White. This insurer does business in Orleans Parish and against whom plaintiff proceeds in direct action.

C. Child Placement Services, Inc., a Louisiana non-profit corporation domiciled in Orleans Parish.

D. DEF Insurance Co. is the insurer providing liability and/or medical payments coverage to Child Placement Services Inc. This insurer does business in Orleans Parish and against whom plaintiff proceeds in direct action.

E. The Department of Social Services is a department of the State of Louisiana, able to be sued under the Constitution and laws of this state, and conducting its duties in Orleans Parish by itself or by its Office of Community Services.

F. GHI Insurance Co. is the insurer providing liability and/or medical payments coverage to the Department of Social Services. This insurer does business in this State and against whom plaintiff proceeds in direct action.

4.

The Department of Social Services, Child Placement Services, Inc., Barbara White and

Charles White owed duties of residential therapeutic foster care to M.M.

5.

Somehow on Sunday, January 28, 1996, while in a bathroom tub in the White TFC home, M.M. contacted scalding hot water. The scalding hot water causing first and second degree burns upon 10% of her body, including second degree burns on her buttocks and vagina, and deep second degree burns to her right leg.

6.

M.M. was damaged by bodily injury, disfigurement, pain and suffering, mental anguish, medical expenses for a 19-day hospitalization and future care, and loss of enjoyment of life.

7.

By reason of her young age and condition, M.M. is free of comparative fault.

8.

Barbara White and Charles White are liable:

A. Strict liability for their ownership of the source of hot water and the means for delivery to the bathroom tub, the hot water heater and its setting at the time of the injury and the child-operable faucets, all of which presented an unreasonable risk of injury to plaintiff.

B. Negligent failure to set and/or maintain and/or monitor the hot water heater below the scalding temperature.

C. Negligent failure to set and/or enforce boundaries.

D. Negligent failure to prevent, forbid and/or enforce plaintiff's operation of the tub's faucets.

E. Negligent failure of supervision of plaintiff and/or the White children.

F. Breach of the standard of care owed by TFC home providers.

G. Maltreatment, abuse, and/or unreasonable discipline.

H. Any other basis of liability proved at trial.

9.

Child Placement Services, Inc. is liable:

A. Vicariously for its agents, Barbara White and Charles White.

B. Negligent failure to provide an adequate and safe placement.

C. Negligent failure to monitor the environmental, health, and safety of the White TFC home.

D. Any other basis of liability proved at trial.

10.

The Department of Social Services is liable:

A. Vicarious liability for its agents, Barbara White, Charles White, and Child Placement Services, Inc. This liability is non-delegable.

B. Negligent failure to provide an adequate and safe placement.

C. Negligent failure to monitor the environmental, health, and safety of the White TFC home.

D. Any other basis of liability proved at trial.

## 11.

Plaintiff demands reasonable compensation for her damages. This demand exceeds the sum required for jury trial. Plaintiff demands jury trial.

WHEREFORE, tutrix Alberta Jones, Esq. for plaintiff M.M. prays that Barbara White, wife of/and Charles White, ABC Insurance Co., Child

Placement Services, Inc., DEF Insurance Co., Department of Social Services, and GHI Insurance Co. be served with this petition and that after due proceedings there be judgment casting defendants liable, jointly and in solido, unto plaintiff for compensatory damages in an amount to be determined by this Honorable Court, together with court costs, legal interest from the date of demand, and all other general and equitable relief.

# CHAPTER 6

Frazier took the suit to the civil court and filed it. He asked the duty judge to seal the record due to juvenile court confidentiality. After this was done, Frazier directed the Civil Sheriff to serve the suit on the Whites at their home in New Orleans East, upon the attorney who was the registered agent for Child Placement Services, Inc., and upon the secretary of the Department of Social Services.

Next, Frazier prepared the paperwork to confirm the tutors in civil court. Although they had been chosen in the Juvenile Court they still had to qualify and take oaths in civil court. This qualification process meant running an ad in the newspaper and otherwise telling Monique's family about the existence of the scalding lawsuit.

When Monique was released from the hospital, the social workers gave her to her paternal grandmother Sarah Thompson even though baby daddy Demetrius Jackson was still in jail. The social workers felt that Lana had not cleaned herself up and was not ready to raise her daughter again. She had given birth to a son. While she did find an apartment in the projects separate from her mother Rose's filthy home, Lana was still drinking and doing coke.

Lana did take an interest in the lawsuit, however. She found out about the lawsuit from Frazier's letter for the tutors. Lana called him and said she was in favor of getting something from the foster parents who had hurt her daughter. She said Monique told her the man Charles White had dunked her in the hot water. She said the hospital did a good job getting the skin to heal, but Monique was not the same as before. Not soft and gently brown like the rest of her, but her scars were tanned and tough. Lana also said the girl limps when she walks. Lana said she would ask Sarah Thompson to bring the girl to the next juvenile court hearing so photographs of the scars could be taken.

Over the next two weeks Frazier was contacted by three attorneys for the defendants. They told Frazier that the

White's homeowners insurer was Allstate Insurance Company, and that Scottsdale Insurance Company insured Child Placement Services, Inc. The Department of Social Services did not have insurance, which was no surprise. The three attorneys each asked for an extra thirty days to investigate and plead to the suit. This request for additional delay was customary. While Frazier preferred to get the suit moving, he approved the additional time upon the condition that the attorneys send him a letter confirming their request and Frazier's approval. Better to be cooperative with opposing counsel at the outset of the suit than to jam them. Perhaps in the future Frazier himself might need a little leeway with a deadline. His ability to cooperate at the outset would be remembered.

Without waiting for the initial answers, Frazier asked the Civil Sheriff to serve an amended copy of the suit upon Allstate Insurance Company, and upon Scottsdale Insurance Company, through their respective registered agents.

Furthermore, Frazier wrote to Children's Hospital for a certified copy of Monique's medical record and the bill. Because the bill had been paid by Medicaid, he also wrote to the state Department of Health and Hospitals to give them notice of the lawsuit and to obtain a copy of their lien.

After about a month Children's replied with a large ream of documents. Children's said it billed Medicaid $17,114.61 for Monique's 19 day stay. Frazier stamped these medical records with serial numbers. It took DHH longer to reply. DHH said the amount actually paid to Children's was $17,114.61, and that DHH had a lien for that amount against any recovery that might be made for Monique.

To complete his initial document collection, Frazier then issued the following requests for information to the defendants:

## PLAINTIFF'S FIRST DISCOVERY

Plaintiff seeks discovery from each of the defendants within 30 days of each answer. Your answers shall be seasonably amended.

INTERROGATORIES TO ALL DEFENDANTS

1.      Please identify those paragraphs of the petition which you admit unconditionally. For each petition paragraph which you deny wholly or in part, state the contrary facts which are the basis of your dispute.

2.      If you contend that plaintiff's injuries were caused by the fault of others, please identify those third persons and state what they did wrong.

3.      Please identify every lay witness you intend to call at trial and state the facts to which they are expected to testify.

4.      Please identify every expert witness you intend to call at trial. Please provide a copy

of each expert's resume. Please provide a copy of every report prepared by each expert or, in the alternative, state all of the facts upon which their opinions are based.

## REQUEST FOR PRODUCTION TO ALLSTATE INSURANCE COMPANY AND SCOTTSDALE INSURANCE COMPANY

Please certify as true, and provide, a copy of each policy or certificate of liability or medical payments insurance in effect on January 28, 1996 insuring Barbara White, Charles White, or Child Placement Services, Inc.

## REQUEST FOR PRODUCTION TO CHILD PLACEMENT SERVICES, INC. AND DEPARTMENT OF SOCIAL SERVICES

Please provide a copy of each document created before January 28, 1996 which mentions Monique Meak and/or Barbara White and Charles White.

# CHAPTER 7

Skinner Auld opened his mail with a scowl. He got a fair amount of mail every day as attorney for Scottsdale Insurance Company. He didn't like having his secretary open the mail because he was afraid she might miss something important. Auld's office was downtown in a high rise building. His firm occupied three floors of the building, and his office was in the corner of the topmost floor. Auld had formed the firm 30 years before when he was a new lawyer, and now he had more than a dozen lawyers working with him.

Auld decorated his office in an Old South theme. Spread across the wall above his credenza was a Civil War battle mural depicting a Confederate charge against Union lines. On another wall he had a framed poster for the Ole Miss Rebels football team. Next to the poster were framed, browning newspaper clippings about the Civil Rights riots at Ole Miss. Auld was a student there at the time and he often regaled visitors with tales of throwing tear gas back at the

National Guard troops sent to enforce integration orders. On another wall Auld kept a primitive painting of plantation life replete with cartoon-like darkies in white clothes stooped over in the cotton fields. You might say Auld was unreconstructed.

He read Monique's suit and the scowl deepened. The suit meant new work, which was welcome, but the allegations against his insured Child Placement Services seemed airtight. The suit had been filed on time. The victim was a young child and the injury was painful and severe. His company probably contributed to the scalding in some way or another. It was not likely that he would get out of the suit without paying something. And, the child's lawyer was asking for a jury trial where he probably planned on whipping up the emotions of the jurors for a big hit. He didn't recognize Frazier's name but he figured, from the quality of the petition, that he was a seasoned litigator.

Auld called Frazier, introduced himself, and asked for an additional thirty days leave to investigate and plead the suit.

But, instead of simply following up with a confirming letter, Auld prepared a motion for Frazier to sign. This motion had two purposes: to show Frazier that Auld would not be led, and to bill his insurer for the extra work. Auld mailed this motion to Frazier and, two days later, sent another letter asking for the identities of the other opposing counsel. Plainly Auld intended to coordinate his response to the suit and discovery with the other attorneys.

# CHAPTER 8

Sarah Thompson called Frazier. She was Monique's paternal grandmother, a sandwich maker in her 40s. She had gotten his letter about the lawsuit, and she had spoken with Lana Meak about getting photographs made of the scars. She said she thought photographs would be a good idea, and that maybe a professional studio should take them. Frazier agreed and located a studio and made an appointment for her.

Next, Frazier was called by her son, Demetrius Jackson. He called collect from the Orleans Parish House of Detention and said he would be there for another five months. He had gotten one of the tutorship letters and wanted to know about Monique's lawsuit. Frazier told him that the suit was just starting and that if Monique won anything, it would take years. Frazier also said that any money won would be controlled by the courts and tutors for Monique's benefit alone. He told Demetrius that no one in the family would get their hands on Monique's money.

In the mail came another letter from Auld. It included an answer for Child Protection Services, Inc. and Scottsdale Insurance Company that merely denied all of the petition allegations. Also, Auld's letter included a copy of the Scottsdale policy, as well as formal discovery requests seeking information about various basic subjects from Monique. Frazier set the discovery aside, knowing other requests would come from the other attorneys and that they could all be answered together with the documents he was collecting. Frazier also prepared the paperwork to confirm the tutors and filed this at court.

The next day Auld called for a 30-day extension on Monique's discovery request, which Frazier granted. The following day Frazier received a letter from Auld confirming the discovery extension. Auld also produced a copy of the CPS contract which said the Whites were not agents of the company. Auld also asked Frazier to copy him with any pleadings filed by the Whites or by the state. Auld was asking

Frazier to act as his secretary, which Frazier ignored. Instead, Frazier sent a copy of the confirmed tutorship to all of the attorneys and Monique's relatives. He called the tutrix and discussed the status of the case, especially the coverage problems with the insurance policies. By various technical reasons, neither Scottsdale nor Allstate promised to insure the Whites as foster parents. This left the Whites in the position of having their own money at risk, and of having to find their own attorney.

In a couple days the photographic studio called saying the proofs were ready to view. Frazier went to the studio, picked out the photos, and ordered six prints of each plus a slide and the negatives. The pictures showed a shadow on Monique's legs from the scarring. These photos would be ready in three weeks. In the meantime, Frazier received general denial answers and more discovery requests from the Whites, Allstate and DSS.

Auld called Frazier, complaining that Monique had not timely answered his discovery. Frazier explained how he was collecting and index stamping the information for all of the attorneys, and that he needed another 15 days to complete the project. Auld granted the extra time, and asked Frazier for a settlement offer, some small amount to get his company out of the suit. Frazier promised to take it up his settlement overture with the tutors.

Frazier next talked with the attorney for the state about the Scottsdale policy and the lowball settlement feeler. Frazier explained that he was not inclined to settle so early or cheaply because Monique had not been fully evaluated for her damages. The state's lawyer said he is sometimes willing to settle these types of cases, but sometimes higher-ups in the administration or legislature will force a case to trial, often for higher than the settlement value.

Next, Frazier talked to the attorney for the Whites. It turns out he is the husband of the presiding judge. He agrees to ask his wife to recuse herself from further involvement in the case, and to transfer the file to another judge. He agrees to send his homeowner's policy and answer Monique's discovery. He says he is not prepared to talk settlement. He agrees to offer the Whites for deposition at a time and place convenient to all attorneys.

Frazier then wrote to all attorneys to confirm the conversations and to decline Auld's offer of an early settlement because Monique's losses had not yet been expertly evaluated.

# CHAPTER 9

The judge did recuse herself and in her place Judge Ethel Gardner was picked to be the new presiding judge. Judge Gardner was about 50 years of age and had sat on the Civil District Court for 15 years. She was one of the first women judges elected to that court, and since that first election no one has run against her. She was even-handed, if not a tad bit imperious, in her secure seat. Before being elected judge, she was an Assistant City Attorney. Her father was a popular former police chief. She is the mother of a child with a learning disability handicap. Judge Gardner wore her dark hair cut short, sported blocky glasses in heavy black frames, and was a bit pale and pudgy for working long hours indoors. She enjoyed using the huge power that Louisiana trial judges have to shape the outcome of cases.

At Monique's trial, Judge Gardner will judge the state and the jury will judge the rest of the defendants. Juries are not trusted to render judgments against the State. Most likely,

Judge Gardner will try to force a settlement because she had a crowded docket, and because settlements avoided the potential embarrassment of appeals. She was known to be generous in good cases.

Frazier's only prior interaction with Judge Gardner did not go well for the judge. Frazier represented a person who had been interdicted (guardianship). However, Frazier dug up a technical defect. Yet, Judge Gardner refused to annul the interdiction, feeling that freedom was not in Frazier's client's best interests. However, the state Supreme Court reversed her, saying she had failed to follow the correct procedure when the interdiction was taken. The stink was so bad the Supreme Court commissioned a state-wide study of interdiction practices and this led to a legislative overhaul. Frazier doubted Judge Gardner carried a grudge, but he wasn't sure.

# CHAPTER 10

Six months after he filed suit, Frazier lumped together all of the discovery requests from the defendants, and serially stamped all of the documents he collected, to prepare this response:

### PLAINTIFF'S CONSOLIDATED ANSWER TO INTERROGATORIES AND RESPONSE TO REQUESTS FOR PRODUCTION

1. Interrogatories and Requests for Production (Feb. 28, 1997) by Child Placement Services, Inc. (CPS)

2. Interrogatories and Requests for Production (May 16, 1997) by Department of Social Services (DSS)

Plaintiff Monique Meak now answers and responds, reserving the right to further amendment and supplementation.

| Number | Description |
| --- | --- |
| 1 – 9 | Photographs circa 3/1/97 |

## DESCRIPTION OF INJURIES

CPS Request for Production #1: Any and all photographs taken of the plaintiff, M.M., which depict the injuries sustained as a result of the incident of January 28, 1996.

DSS Interrogatory #1: Describe in detail the injuries received by M.M. in the accident set forth in the petition.

DSS Interrogatory #3: Please state whether or not any of the injuries claimed are of a permanent nature, and if so, which of said injuries are the basis of the claim.

DSS Request for Production #2: Copies of any and all photographs of the plaintiff with relation to the injuries allegedly incurred as a result of the accident complained of in the petition for damage.

**See photo exhibits 1 - 9. See descriptions of injuries as contained in those exhibits 000015 - 000079 dated on or after January 28, 1996; those exhibits 000080 - 000225 dated on or after January 28, 1996; exhibits 000226 - 000451; and exhibits 000658 - 000663. Since the photos of Monique Meak were made more than one year after the incident, the visible scars are believed to be permanent.**

WITNESSES

CPS Interrogatory #1: What is the name, residential address, residential telephone number, and employment address of each person known by plaintiff and/or plaintiff's attorney or anyone charged with the responsibility of caring for the plaintiff who: (a) was a witness to the incident of January 28, 1996, (b) has personal knowledge of the facts and circumstances surrounding the incident of January 28, 1996, (c) or was in the home of Barbara and Charles White when the incident of January 28, 1996 occurred.

CPS Interrogatory #5: Please state the name, address and telephone number of each person who supposedly has personal knowledge that Barbara White or Charles White were guilty of "maltreatment, neglect, abuse, and/or unreasonable discipline" while functioning as foster parents.

**See DSS/OCS investigation as contained in those exhibits 000015 - 000079 and/or**

**000080 - 000225 dated on or after January 28, 1996.**

MEDICAL TREATMENT - RECORDS AND BILLS

CPS Interrogatory #2: Please state the name, address and telephone number of each doctor, surgeon, physician, psychiatrist, psychologist, or social worker who has examined and/or treated the plaintiff, M.M., for any ailment, injury or condition arising as a result of the incident of January 28, 1996.

CPS Interrogatory #3: With respect to each medical provider listed in your answer to Interrogatory #2, please provide the following information: (a) a short description of the injury, ailment, or condition for which he examined and/or treated M.M.; (b) the date or dates of each occasion when he examined and/or treated M.M.;

(c) the amount of money charged by him for medical services rendered.

CPS Interrogatory #4: Please state the name and address of each hospital or clinic at which the plaintiff, M.M., was treated for any ailment, injury or condition arising as a result of the incident of January 28, 1996.

CPS Request for Production #2: Any medical bills, medical reports, hospital records, or other medical documentation of any medical providers who examined and/or treated M.M., for any injuries sustained as a result of the incident of January 28, 1996.

DSS Interrogatory #2: Please state the name and address of each hospital, doctor, physical therapist, or other medical professional who treated M.M., a description of each treatment rendered by the various medical professionals, including whether the treatment was rendered at the doctor's offices, at home, or in the hospital.

DSS Interrogatory #4: Has M.M. received any physical therapy? If so, who rendered such treatment, describe the treatment and state the date you received such treatment and the cost of said treatment.

DSS Interrogatory #5: Please itemize, by name and address, all medical bills paid or incurred in connection with the accident described in the petition, including but not limited to, the cost of the ambulance service, doctor bills, x-rays, hospital expenses, nursing expenses, medicines, surgical apparatus or other costs.

DSS Request for Production #1: Copies of any and all medical reports, from all doctors, hospitals, physical therapist or other medical professionals treating the plaintiff for injuries incurred as a result of the alleged accident complained of in the petition for damages.

**See medical records as contained in those exhibits 000015 - 000079 dated on or after January 28, 1996; those exhibits 000080 - 000225 dated on or after January 28, 1996; exhibits 000226 - 000451; and exhibits 000658 - 000663. Total medical costs are unknown at this time, but are believed to exceed $17,000.00.**

DAMAGES

DSS Interrogatory #6: Please itemize any other expenses or financial loses which have been paid or incurred or which you attribute to the accident described in the petition.

DSS Interrogatory #7: Please state whether or not you are claiming as an element of damages, future medical expenses. If so, state the amount claimed and the basis upon which you compute the amount.

DSS Interrogatory #8: If you sustained any additional losses as a result of the incident complained of, other than those covered by the proceeding interrogatories, please state nature and amount of each loss; the date thereof, and the names and addresses of any person to who any money so claimed as an additional loss was paid.

DSS Interrogatory #9: State whether you are claiming mental pain and anguish as an element or damage, and if so, the amount and basis from which you compute said amount.

**See exhibits, and see petition. Total medical costs and other specials are not known. Future medicals unknown. General damages exceed the $50,000.00 awarded in Edwards v. Pelican State Mut. Ins. Co., 95-253**

(La. App. 3 Cir. 5/31/95); 657 So.2d 440 (five-year-old swallowed caustic solution; esophagus and stomach burns healed rapidly).

# CHAPTER 11

Next, Frazier reviewed the homeowner's policy provided by Allstate. It excluded personal injuries to residents of the insured's household. It excluded personal injuries resulting from operating a business in the home. It excluded personal injuries caused by intentional acts. Frazier decided Allstate will probably move for summary judgment to be dismissed from the case. It would be hard to defeat such a motion. Frazier advised the tutors that he would leave it to the Whites to battle to keep Allstate in. The Whites had a greater incentive to keep Allstate in than Monique did since she still had two other deep pockets, Scottsdale and DSS.

Ten months after suit was filed Frazier began contacting the other lawyers about setting up depositions. A deposition is a formal question and answer session done for discovery of information, but conducted under oath just as if the testimony was being taken at trial. Frazier quickly learned that he had to choose dates more than three months in advance in order to avoid conflicts with the four other attorneys' schedules. Frazier attempted to schedule the depositions of the Whites, of the Children's Hospital ER doctor, of the representatives of DSS, and of the representatives of CPS. He prepared lengthy notices describing the topics to be covered in the depositions, and sent theses to all counsel.

The other lawyers asked that Monique be made available for deposition and viewing, too. Frazier resisted because Monique was too young, too mentally challenged, and too emotionally unstable to predict what she might say. Monique could easily hurt her own case and not intend to do so. Nor should she be made to exhibit her scars to the attorneys because of undue embarrassment and their lack of medical training. The tutors agreed the deposition and viewing should be opposed. Also Monique's grandmother, Sarah Thompson, felt Monique should not be made to appear in the same room as the Whites. Thus, when Skinner Auld noticed Monique's deposition, Frazier filed a motion to quash.

Upon reviewing the motion to quash, Judge Gardner ordered:

> IT IS ORDERED THAT defendants Barbara White, Charles White, Allstate Insurance Company, Child Placement Services, Inc., Scottsdale Insurance Co., and Department of Social Services shall show cause, in <u>closed hearing</u> in chambers on the 13th day of February, 1998 at 10:00 o'clock why plaintiff should not be granted a protective order with regard to the deposition testimony of the minor, Monique Meak, in the following particulars:
>
> 1. that Monique Meak first be determined to be competent and, if so, that the deposition be conducted immediately afterward by the Court upon submitted questions;
>
> 2. that Charles White and Barbara White (but not their counsel) be excluded from the competency

hearing and any subsequent deposition of Monique Meak; and

3. that Monique Meak, pre-trial, not be required to display the scars of her burn (on her right thigh and buttocks) to any non-medical personnel.

When the time arrived to begin the December depositions, the defense attorneys balked at producing any of their parties until the judge ruled on Monique's motion to quash. Thus, only the deposition of the ER doctor was taken. The depositions of the representatives of DSS and CPS were rescheduled for another eight weeks. Coincidentally, DSS and CPS would be deposed on the second anniversary of the scalding. The Whites' depositions were continued without a new date.

In summary, the DSS and CPS depositions revealed these facts: DSS hired CPS to recruit and train foster parents, including therapeutic foster care parents. The Whites had previously served as foster parents to two or three children at a time. They had even adopted one child after receiving a post-adoption subsidy. They were recruited by CPS to become therapeutic foster care parents for Monique. TFC paid more for 24-hour supervision.

As a part of the recruiting process, the Whites' home was inspected. As to the hot water in the bathtub, the CPS manual said:

> **The hot water accessible to the children does not exceed 120 degrees Fahrenheit at the outlet. (This does not apply to faucets that can mix hot and cold water.)**

Thus, when DSS and CPS inspected the White home, it was observed that the bathtub had one hot water valve and one cold water valve leading into a common faucet. DSS and CPS assumed this met the manual requirement without anyone actually getting off the couch and measuring the temperature of the hot-only flow. DSS contended the CPS manual was misleading and vague because what DSS wanted was for the hot water to be tested except where the faucets were connected to an anti-scald device that automatically mixed the hot and cold water. Three months after the "inspection" DSS and CPS first learned the Whites' bathtub had scalding water when Monique lay sobbing in Children's Hospital.

Frazier conducted extensive legal research about a child's comparative fault and about the liability of foster parents and the state. He learned that very young children do not get blamed for their own injuries. He learned that the State was liable for whatever damages the foster parents caused as a matter of fiduciary liability – the law required the State to provide for the foster child's needs, so any wrong then committed to the child was ultimately the State's responsibility. Frazier suggested to the tutors that he should file for summary judgment on both of these two issues because of the huge advantage which would be gained if successful, and because just filing the motion would educate the defendants and encourage them to fight among themselves. Thus, Frazier prepared and filed the following motions and set them on the same day as the motion to quash Monique's deposition:

## MEMORANDUM IN SUPPORT OF PLAINTIFF'S MOTION FOR PARTIAL SUMMARY JUDGMENT

Plaintiff Monique Meak contends there are no material facts at issue, and thus moves for two partial summary judgments.

## INCAPABLE OF COMPARATIVE FAULT

On January 27, 1996, the date of her alleged injury, Monique Meak was 4½ years old. See birth certificate attached to motion to quash deposition.

Prior to her alleged injury, Monique Meak was diagnosed with fetal alcohol syndrome, developmentally delayed, moderate to severe language disorder, and moderate to severe delays in articulation skills. See exhibits attached to motion to quash.

Six months after the scalding burn, Monique Meak's kindergarten individualized placement evaluation (IEP) found "significant cognitive impairment" and "mild to moderate deficits in adaptive behavior," a high level of motor behavior, an inability "to concentrate on any task for an adequate amount of time," and, contrasted to her chronological age of five years, an overall mental and developmental age was just 25 months, including a 19-months score in communication skills. See exhibits attached to motion to quash.

Eight months after the scalding burn, a second evaluation said Monique Meak demonstrated "a significant delay in cognitive functioning" by performing at the 35 months, that she was "not compliant for administration of all test items as she was active and highly distractible," that she "was not compliant for complete administration of the Expressive Communication subscale. Her high activity level and impulsivity adversely affected her ability to adequately perform tasks presented," that she had these weaknesses: remaining seated, attending to the tasks presented, ability to tell about remote events, ability to describe a procedure or event, and that "her communication difficulties adversely affect her interaction with peers and adults in that it draws attention to itself." See exhibits attached to motion to quash.

## ARGUMENT

In her petition, Monique Meak alleged she was free of fault due to her age or condition. Each defendant has denied the allegation. This Court should declare that Monique Meak was incapable of comparative fault.

The capacity of the parties is part of the comparative fault evaluation:

In assessing the nature of the conduct of the parties, various factors may influence the degree of fault assigned, including: ... (4) the capacities of the actor, whether superior or inferior ....

Watson v. State Farm Fire and Cas. Ins. Co., 469 So.2d 967 (La. 1985).

Whether a child had the capacity to indulge in gross disregard of his own safety in the face of known and perceived danger must be measured by his age, maturity, background, inherent intelligence, and capacity to evaluate the circumstances. Demery v. Housing Auth., 96-1024 (La.App. 4 Cir. 2/12/97); 689 So.2d 659. **Age seven is the "bright line"**; even older children may be excused depending on their particular circumstances. Moore v. State Farm Mut. Auto. Ins., 499 So.2d 146 at footnote 1 (La.App. 2 Cir. 1986).

The caselaw provides several instances of very young children being assessed **ZERO** fault due to their ages:

- **a 2-year-old** who wandered from a yard into a highway, McFarland v. Industrial Helicopters, 502 So.2d 593 (La.App. 3 Cir. 1987).

- **a 3-year-old** burned by gasoline stored near a hot water heater, Toups v. Sears, Roebuck and Co., Inc., 507 So.2d 809 (La. 1987).

- **a 5-year-old** who rolled his tricycle down a driveway into a street, Smith v. Trahan, 398 So.2d 572 (La.App. 1st Cir. 1980).

- **a 6-year-old** injured while playing tag in tall grass, Fusilier v. Northbrook Excess and Surplus, Inc., 471 So.2d 761 (La.App. 3rd Cir. 1985), writ denied, 472 So.2d 918 (La. 1985).

- **a 6-year-old** injured by jumping off a porch while playing tag, Bordelon v. Pelican State Mut. Ins., 599 So.2d 511 (La.App. 3 Cir. 1992).

- **a 7-year-old** who was cut by a nail in pile of lumber while playing tag, Jackson v. Jones, 224 La. 403, 69 So.2d 729 (1954).

Monique Meak was 4½ years old when she was scalded. The child was also impulsive, hyperactive, and had a diminished intellectual capacity. By her age alone -- and by her condition -- Monique Meak was legally incapable of comparative negligence in her injury. As a matter of law, Monique Meak is entitled to summary judgment declaring her free of comparative fault.

## DSS, AS FIDUCIARY, IS 100% LIABLE

The Department of Social Services ("DSS") secretary is the "legal custodian of any child placed with the department by a court of law," R.S. 36:474(B)(5). Her custodial rights and duties are exercised by DSS's Office of Community Services, ("OCS"), R.S. 36:471(C)(1).

At the time of her scalding, DSS had legal custody of Monique Meak. DSS/OCS put her into the foster care placement where she was scalded. See the attached copies of orders from the Orleans Parish Juvenile Court.

Three weeks after the scalding, a status letter from OCS to the Juvenile Court reported, "Monique was first placed in a therapeutic foster home, with Barbara White. However, while living at this home, she sustained first and second degree burns, and was admitted to Children's Hospital. This incident is still under investigation by our Child Protection Unit." Exhibit 000045, attached. The letter was jointly signed by OCS supervisor Priscilla Bruce and by OCS caseworker Joyce Allen. **The statement is offered as an admission against interest, C.E. 801(D)(2)(c) or C.E. 801(D)(3)(a).** The Juvenile

Court approved the disclosure of its orders and court letters in this action, Exhibits 000013 - 000014. Ms. Allen testified about the court letter:

Q.     What questions were asked of you in the court proceeding?

A.     A lot of questions that really dealt with CPI, and I couldn't really answer them because I hadn't done the investigation.

Q.     What was the - who was being charged? What was the - on the agenda of the court that day for you to be testifying?

A.     I was reporting to the judge. When we go in and submit our court letters, we also - after you've submitted your court letter, if you don't have time to write an addendum, you do testimony as to if there have been any changes in the case.

Q.     Okay. And you were questioned by the judge or by an attorney?

A.     By the judge.

Q.     And what did you tell the judge with respect to the burning incident?

A.     I just related to Judge Green Monique's response to me about how she was burned.

**Joyce Allen as DSS 1441-1442 designee, deposition pp. 98 - 99, attached.**

One month after the scalding, DSS's Child Protection investigator found Monique Meak had been scalded in the foster home of Charles and Barbara White either through negligent supervision, or by an immersion inconsistent with self-inflicted or accidental injury. Exhibit LA1 - LA3, attached. The report was jointly prepared by OCS investigator Carolyn Black and her supervisor, Darlene Jones. **The statement is offered as an admission against interest, C.E. 801(D)(2)(c) or C.E. 801(D)(3)(a).** This exhibit was authenticated by Darlene Jones:

Q. I am going to show you documents that I have marked as LA-1 through LA-24.

A. Okay.

Q. Can you identify what those are, please.

A.     This is an investigative packet prepared by
Carolyn Black regarding the investigation of the
foster home of Barbara White and Charles White,
involving an incident in which Monique Meak
sustained burns.

**Darlene Jones DSS 1441-1442 designee,
deposition p. 30, attached.**

ARGUMENT

The Department of Social Services has a

non-delegable, fiduciary duty to care for, and

protect, its wards.  When the State's apparatus for

care and protection fails, causing injury to the

foster child, the State is 100% liable to the child

for the breach of fiduciary duty.  This duty arises

in a social contract, rooted in vital public policy

and embodied by two statutes:

"Legal custody" means the right to have physical
custody of the child and **to determine where and
with whom the child shall reside**; to exercise the
rights and **duty to protect**, train, and discipline
the child; the authority to consent to major
medical, psychiatric, and surgical treatment; **and
to provide the child with** food, **shelter**,
education, and ordinary medical care, all subject

to any residual rights possessed by the child's parents.

Ch.C. art. 116(12), emphasis added.

When a child adjudicated in need of care is referred to the Department of Social Services for care and treatment, such care and treatment is to be provided by the department either through facilities and programs operated by the department or through contractual arrangements pursuant to R.S. 15:1083 and 1084 or through purchase of service arrangements for which the department provides funding, and **the child shall be assigned to the exclusive custody of the department** rather than to a particular institution or facility. **The department shall have sole authority over the placement, care**, treatment, or any other considerations deemed necessary from the resources that are available for children judicially committed to the department.

Ch.C. art. 672(A), emphasis supplied. The State may not delegate its custodial responsibility, even though it hires foster parents to provide care on the state's behalf. Smith v. State, Div. of Fam. Ser., 452 So.2d 388 (La.App. 3 Cir. 1984); State in Interest of LW, 27,689 (La.App. 2 Cir. 9/27/95); 661 So.2d 614.

As a matter of vital public policy, the State's ultimate responsibility to adequately shelter and protect its foster children is **non-delegable trust**. By this social contract the State is liable as fiduciary to its foster children for the torts committed by the State's employees, agents, and independent contractors. Thus, the State as fiduciary was liable to a foster child beaten to death by a foster parent, <u>Vonner v. State, Dept. of Public Welfare</u>, 273 So.2d 252 (La. 1973) (specifically citing the statutes antecedent to Children's Code arts. 116(12) and 672(A)). Similarly, the State as fiduciary was liable to a foster child who was shot by a foster parent's natural child with a pistol the foster parent had inadequately secured, <u>Cathey v. Bernard</u>, 467 So.2d 9 (La.App. 1 Cir. 1985).

The Court is urged to view the State's own OCS court letter and Child Protection investigation as admissions against interest. The court letter says the injury occurred in the foster parents' home. The CPI report found the scalding occurred through negligent supervision, or by an immersion inconsistent with self-inflicted or accidental injury. By these findings, the State described the failure of the apparatus it selected for Monique Meak's care and protection. These findings, made by authorized agents of the State acting in the scope of their duties, are admissions against the State's interest. The State should be held to the consequences of its admissions against interest, and this Court should declare that DSS is 100% liable, as a fiduciary, for Monique Meak's injuries.

The Court is not being called upon to assess comparative fault of the foster parents, or of DSS's foster parent provider, Child Protection Services, Inc. Perhaps the State can prove a right of contribution or indemnity. But, at this time, Monique Meak is entitled to partial summary judgment against DSS alone.

# CHAPTER 12

As expected, Allstate opposed the amended petition by pleading its policy exclusions, arguing that it owed Monique nothing because it did not provide coverage to the Whites. Allstate filed a motion for summary judgment to get out of the suit, and set it for the same date as plaintiff's motions. Frazier told the tutors that "pursuing the homeowner's insurance in this case is probably a loser. Better to let the Whites fight this one -- they have more to lose than Monique since Monique has CPS and the State as deep pockets."

Just before the February hearing was to take place, Frazier was called by Skinner Auld's office. Auld had broken his leg and wanted the hearing continued. Frazier was disappointed at the delay but said he understood, and that he would prepare the paperwork to move the date of all motions into April. He then called the Court and all attorneys and cleared April 3, 1998 as available for Judge Gardner to hear the motions.

Frazier and the tutrix took a king cake to Sarah Thompson's home where they met with Monique and her relatives. They explained why Monique would probably be ordered by the judge to go to court to show that she was not capable of testifying on her own behalf.

In preparation for the April 3rd hearing, Frazier made notes summarizing all of the parties' arguments:

<u>MOTION TO QUASH DEPOSTION</u>

Age 4.5 at injury, now age 6.5

UNDISPUTED fetal alcohol syndrome, developmentally delayed, moderate to severe language disorder, and moderate to severe delays in articulation skills.

UNDISPUTED two school evaluations show significant cognitive impairment with mental age of three years, inability to stay focused, highly distractible, non-compliance with testing procedure, language and communication problems, difficulty remaining seated, difficulty understanding negatives, difficulty relating remote events, difficulty describing a procedure or event.

Judge should interview Monique -- COURT'S SOUND DISCRETION – <u>Watermier</u> says balance the child's best interests by testing competency in chambers.

Auld says let Monique be deposed under judge's supervision, cites no cases. <u>Watermier</u> says court should conduct deposition upon submitted questions.

Whites want to attend Monique's deposition, and Auld wants them there, too. Cites no cases, says no deliberate acts were alleged. <u>Watermier</u> approves evicting parties if their attorneys have right to ask questions and the parties are available for consultation. Right to assist counsel balanced against child's best interest. Even though the Whites sat with Monique at the hospital, all the more reason the child should be isolated against undue influences.

Auld want to view Monique in her panties. Cites no case. No, not a medical person. C.C.P. arts. 1463-1464.

## INCAPABLE OF COMPARATIVE FAULT

Age 7 is bright line -- NO ONE REBUTTED. Freedom from comparative fault was pleaded in petition. All defendants denied it.

Allstate says this issue is not dispositive of a claim or a party, so not in the scope of summary judgment, citing 1994 and 1995 cases. Fails to address the changes made in the 1997 revision: ACT NO. 483 of 1997, effective July 1, 1997 allows issue preclusion by summary judgment. C.C.P. 966 (E).

## DSS, AS FIDUCIARY, IS 100% LIABLE

DSS cites no case against fiduciary liability, saying only that fault by the foster parents, the Whites, has not been proven. Auld adopts the DSS argument. However, no one opposed with evidence. No one gave an affidavit exculpating the Whites, so this rebuttal argument lacks evidentiary support and does not prevail, C.C.P. art. 966(C). No material issue was created.

DSS says its employees' statements are hearsay. But admissions against interest are not hearsay, C.Evid. art. 801D.

DSS says Allen's statement to the Juvenile Court, that the burns happened in the White home, is something she learned from another, p. 2. As such, this statement is a relational admission, 801(D)(3)(a) or an authorized admission, 801(D)(2)(c). An admission in another suit is an extrajudicial admission and is admissible as evidence, Cross v. Cutter Biological, 94-1477 (La.App. 4 Cir. 5/29/96); 676 So.2d 131.

DSS does not address Jones's CPI conclusion that Monique was scalded due to the negligent supervision of the Whites. This statement is a relational admission, 801(D)(3)(a).

DSS attacks Jones' CPI conclusion that Monique was scalded due to an immersion inconsistent with self-inflicted or accidental injury due to her reliance upon expert medical opinion, citing McCoy. But McCoy is not followed in Fourth Circuit, particularly where the expert physician has personally examined the party whose health is at issue, Powers v. Tucker, 29190 p. 7 at footnote 1 (La.App. 2 Cir. 2/26/97); 690 So.2d 922 citing three Fourth Cir cases.

DSS says ruling for Monique will have a chilling effect on CPI investigations. No evidence given for this. It must be presumed that public officers will properly discharge their offices. How can DSS say if judge finds DSS liable then DSS employees will breach their investigations of foster care?

# CHAPTER 13

All of the lawyers, including Auld with a cast on his leg, were present for the April 3rd hearing in Judge Gardner's chambers. She had already reviewed the pleadings and arguments filed by counsel, and let them orally argue their motions and oppositions. Then Judge Gardner ruled on the motions orally, and directed Frazier to reduce her orders to a writing consented to by all counsel:

## ORDER

Set for hearing on April 3, 1998 were plaintiff's Motion for Quash, plaintiff's Motion for Partial Summary Judgment, and Allstate's Motion for Summary Judgment. The undersigned counsel appeared and argued. Then the Court ruled as follows:

IT IS ORDERED: regarding plaintiff's motion to quash her own deposition, that the child and her custodian Mrs. Sarah Thompson, or

Mrs. Thompson's designee, shall appear before the Court for competency examination at <u>11:00 a.m. on Friday, June 19, 1998</u>. Not later than one week prior to that date, all parties may file suggested questions relevant to determine the child's competence. The competency exam shall be conducted by the Court, and recorded by the court reporter, with the cost of recording and transcription to be cast by the Court at the close of the examination. The parties shall not attend the competency exam, but their counsel may attend, and shall be afforded the opportunity to raise any objection to the procedure or to the decision. If at the end of the competency hearing the Court determines that Monique Meak is competent to be deposed, then the Court will determine what protections, if any, are necessary for the taking of her deposition. The deposition will not be taken immediately following the competency exam.

IT IS ORDERED: plaintiff's motion for a protective order is granted. Monique Meak shall not exhibit her scars to non-medical personnel. Plaintiff shall share photographs of her scars, and shall submit to examination by a sole physician designated by all defendants.

IT IS ORDERED: plaintiff's motion for partial summary judgment to find no fault by Monique Meak is denied for the want of any affirmative plea of comparative fault by any defendant.

IT IS ORDERED: plaintiff's motion for partial summary judgment, to find the Department of Social Services 100% liable as a fiduciary to Monique Meak, is denied as untimely because the State's admissions alone are not sufficient proof of the fault of the Whites or Child Placement Services, Inc. which has yet to be determined.

IT IS FURTHER ORDERED: that Allstate's motion for summary judgment regarding the coverage exclusions in the Whites' homeowner's policy is denied, with the Whites' having raised a material issue of fact about the child's residency by swearing in an affidavit that they had not decided to permanently house Monique Meak.

# CHAPTER 14

Frazier reported the outcome of the hearing to the tutors. He said, despite the technical losses, that it was clear to Judge Gardner and the attorneys that Monique would not share in the blame for the accident, and that the DSS was her deep pocket. He told the tutrix that Monique had been ordered to appear before Judge Gardner on June 19, 1988 with her grandmother or representative, and that the tutrix should also appear at the competency hearing. Frazier called Sarah Thompson and told her she or someone she selected had been ordered to bring Monique to court on June 19th.

On the day of the competency hearing Monique appeared at court in a shirt and slacks with her paternal aunt Ronda Thompson. As ordered, the competency hearing was held in Judge Gardner's chambers. Everybody squeezed into the judge's office with Monique perched on Frazier's lap in front of the judge.

Judge Gardner asked Monique the questions submitted by Frazier and Auld. The questions were:

1. How old are you?

2. In what year were you born?

3. Where does your father live?

4. What does your father do for a living?

5. Where does your mother live?

6. What does your mother do for a living?

7. Where does your grandmother Sarah live?

8. What does she do for a living?

9. Why were you living with your grandmother?

10. How do you help your grandmother at home?

11. How many brothers and sisters do you have?

12. How old are they?

13. What is the name of your school?

14. What time do you go to school?

15. What time do you come home from school?

16. What subjects do you take at school?

17. Who takes you to school?

18. What is your favorite color?

19. What is your favorite TV show?

20. I told you my name when we started. What is my name?

21. Do you know what the truth is?

22. Is it bad to say something that is not true?

23. If I ask you to always tell me the truth, will you do it?

24. What color is my dress?

25. Suppose I tell you that my (true color) dress is (another color). Now tell me, what color is my dress?

After listening to Monique's responses, Judge Gardner ruled her to be incompetent to be deposed or to testify at trial. She further ruled that Monique would not attend her own trial and would not expose her scars to the jury. If the defense attorneys agreed on a doctor, or on a photographer, then Monique would have to show her scars to them.

The effect of finding Monique incompetent, and forbidding her from attending trial, was that, by one hearsay exception or another, all of her out-of-court statements about how the scalding happened will probably be admitted at trial. The Whites and a CPS worker will testify that Monique told them she turned the water on herself. On the other hand, an OCS social worker and Sarah Thompson will say that Monique told them that Charles White put her in the bathtub. She said the same thing to her mother, but Lana had too many negatives to put on the stand. On a positive note, keeping Monique out of the courtroom will prevent her from causing an embarrassing incident, such as greeting the Whites which might happen due to her attachment disorder, or incontinence or a tantrum.

# CHAPTER 15

In the meantime, over the last eight months while the various motions were pending, Frazier hired forensic sociologist Dr. Edward Morton, of LSU Medical Center's Psychiatry Research Unit, as an expert to review and report on Monique's injuries. From the outset Dr. Morton was interested in whether Monique had suffered a loss of marital worth, and whether she would need long term psychiatry to deal with the scalding and scaring issues.

To assist Dr. Morton, Frazier supplied him with a copy of all of the documents produced to the attorneys. Next he coordinated a home visit with Sarah Thompson on her day off. Frazier met Dr. Morton, Monique, and Sarah Thompson at the Thompson home. After this, Frazier coordinated visits with Monique's parents, Lana Meak and Demetrius Jackson, and with Monique's special education teacher. Dr. Morton also asked Frazier to arrange a visit with grandmother Rose Meak at the filthy home from which DSS took Monique. When

Frazier called Sarah Thompson, he found out that she and Monique and Demetrius Jackson had moved to another rented house on Claiborne Street in New Orleans. Frazier supplemented the discovery answers by disclosing the new addresses, and by disclosing the hire of Dr. Morton, the expert.

When Frazier spoke with mother Lana Meak, she told him that she wanted to get her daughter back from Sarah Thompson. She said she had her own home now, and was ready to care for her child unlike her father, Demetrius Jackson, who was living with another woman and who favored another daughter. Frazier told Lana to contact her Juvenile Court attorney and, that as child's counsel, he would not oppose whoever the judge decided would give Monique the best home. Lana agreed to meet with Dr. Morton.

Dr. Morton provided Frazier with a list of questions for the competency exam, which he forwarded to all counsel and Judge Gardner. The school board cooperated by supplying

Monique's special education and disciplinary folders, which were stamped with serial numbers and copied to all counsel and Dr. Morton. So far, Frazier had supplied four attorneys and his expert with 1,587 pages of documents.

About this time Lana Meak called Frazier again to ask how she could get custody of Monique, saying that she was concerned about the girl not being supervised by Sarah Thompson and about her having injured her leg. Frazier again told her to contact her Juvenile Court lawyer.

Over the next two months Frazier made several attempts to call Sarah Thompson and Demetrius Jackson but without reply. Finally, he drove to the Thompson home where he found Sarah and Monique. Monique appeared well and cared for, but she had fresh scars on her face and left arm. These scars looked like scab-picked mosquito bites. Sarah Thompson said they were scars from a fight Monique had with a neighbor boy last week. Sarah said Monique gets in fights often. When Frazier asked Monique if she fights because her feelings get hurt, she said yes. Frazier explained to Sarah what was going on the in the case and about Dr. Morton's progress on Monique's behalf. Dr. Morton said Monique was transitioning from hyperactive-cute to hyperactive-aggressive.

Two months later Monique received a five-day suspension from school for disrupting her class and for walking out of class. Sarah Thompson requested Frazier's help in getting Monique seen by a psychiatrist. Frazier coordinated an appointment with her and the LSU Medical School Child Psychiatry Clinic.

In January 1989, Frazier received Dr. Morton's report. The expert said he could not detect anything currently wrong with Monique that could be attributed to the scalding. Nor did Dr. Morton say whether Monique would suffer future problems. Clearly Frazier needed a new expert.

# CHAPTER 16

While Frazier was working with Dr. Morton, he also kept busy with the defendants and their lawyers. In October 1998, almost three years since the scalding, the Whites' home was inspected and the Whites were deposed.

Barbara White met the attorneys at her home for the inspection. Frazier brought a kitchen thermometer and a camera to the home inspection. He took photos of the hot water heater and its control box. The hot water heater was switched to HIGH. Then, the attorneys were led by Mrs. White to the upstairs bathroom. There was a hook and eye latch high on the door. The bathtub was located about six feet directly above the water heater. Frazier sampled the hot water. It read 135 degrees Fahrenheit.

Next, the attorneys assembled for the Whites' depositions at their attorney's office. In summary, Barbara White testified that she and her husband Charles were foster parents for about three years. They kept two to three foster children at a time, at $850 per month per child. They had even adopted one foster child. After CPS certified them as TFC parents, the Whites were paid $1,250 per month to give 24-hour care to Monique. Before putting Monique in the home, CPS did not fully explain to the Whites the extent of Monique's problems. Yet, even though the Whites discovered Monique was incontinent and taking off her diaper, eating out of the garbage can, hyperactive, breaking things, and injuring herself, they never asked OCS or CPS to remove the child. For three months Barbara White dutifully filled out reports documenting Monique's poor behavior, as well as critical incident reports when some form of correction was used. One of the things this four-year-old did, about a week before the scalding, was swing a broom and dent the fabric screen on the family's big screen TV.

On the morning of the scalding, Barbara said her family had gone to church. They came home and were cleaning house because a social worker was expected that afternoon.

Barbara noticed her son was starting to have an asthma attack so she decided to give him a quick bath upstairs and then to take him into the master bedroom for a nebulizer treatment. Monique was at the bottom of the stairs, asking to be bathed also.     Barbara told her no, but Monique kept insisting. Barbara asked Charles to keep an eye on her.   Charles was about to vacuum the front room at the bottom of the stairs. Barbara unlatched the hook and eye latch on the bathroom door, ran a bath for her son, drained the tub when done, then went into her room to run the noisy nebulizer machine.  She forgot to re-latch the bathroom door.  Though she could see the upper staircase landing, she never saw Monique come up the stairs.  Perhaps Monique went in the bathroom while her other son blocked her view by standing in the bedroom doorway.  She never heard the tub water because of the noisy nebulizer machine, but she did hear Monique scream.  Before she could jump up and cross into the bathroom, Charles appeared holding Monique.  Barbara wrapped her in a sheet and they took her to the hospital. When Barbara came home that night, she saw Monique's dirty diaper on the floor next to the bathtub. Barbara spent several days sitting with Monique at the hospital until the State began an abuse/neglect investigation of the scalding.

In turn, Charles White testified that he drove a public transit bus and, on the Sunday in question, his wife Barbara told him to watch Monique to keep her from going upstairs, but he turned his back while vacuuming and she got away. He did not leave the front room. He did not hear the water run in the tub. When he heard Monique scream he ran upstairs. Charles said when he reached the tub, the hot water was still flowing out of the faucet. He said Monique was standing scrunched back into the corner of the bathtub, at the deepest spot between the faucet and the wall. He was emphatic that Monique was standing in the scalding water. Charles said he grabbed her, swung her away from the hot water, and carried her into Barbara's bedroom.    Charles denied dunking

Monique.

# CHAPTER 17

While waiting on Dr. Morton's report, Frazier was called by Skinner Auld who wanted to talk settlement for CPS and Scottsdale. Auld said his people are not the ones who scalded Monique, and that CPS is a good company that does good things for needy people. He said he expects to escape liability and offered $15,000 merely as a token to end the litigation.

The attorney for DSS said he might be able to sell Auld on splitting a $70,000 settlement, but also said getting DHH to waive its medicals lien would be nearly impossible.

Frazier discussed these settlement offers with tutrix who rejected them as too low. Next, Frazier scheduled a status conference with Judge Fredrickson, the tutorship judge, to see what he thought a fair settlement might be. According to Judge Fredrickson, when a four-year-old suffers second degree scalding burns in a foster home, and undergoes debridement for 19 days, and the medical specials exceed

$17,000, the case should settle for around $100,000 and perhaps more if future harm is uncovered.

In late March 1999 Frazier wrote to all opposing counsel that he had authority from the tutrix to settle for $125,000 with waiver of DHH's medical lien. Frazier also consented to mediation.

Six weeks later, in mid-May 1999, the attorney for DSS said he will agree to mediation as a way to force Auld and CPS to honor the indemnity clause of their contract with DSS. In turn, Auld sticks with the same $15,000 he offered three months earlier, calling it "lagniappe."

The attorneys appeared in court and picked a trial date of March 13-15, 2000. Judge Gardner's office issued a pre-trial order containing a calendar of cut-off dates.

# CHAPTER 18

Frazier was not satisfied with Dr. Morton's inability to forecast Monique's future needs due to the scalding. He located another expert, a pediatric burn psychologist from the Shriner's Burn Hospital in Galveston, Texas named Dr. Wanda Carney. Dr. Carney was called "the grandmother of burn survivor psychology." She had a 14-page resume stuffed with publications. She nearly single-handedly invented the specialty of psychological pain management and recovery for burn victims. Dr. Carney was well-recommended by other burn litigation plaintiff attorneys. After talking with Dr. Carney, it was plain that she considered Monique to be a person and not a meal ticket. Frazier agreed to hire her at $150 per hour, $200 per hour for testimony, and paid her a $1,000 retainer. He supplied Dr. Carney with the same 1,587 serially-numbered documents he had given the other attorneys and Dr. Morton, as well as a copy of Dr. Morton's report. He also sent Dr. Carney this letter.

Your focus will be the probable future psychological effects and needs of Monique Meak, born July 17, 1991, resulting from a scalding burn suffered on January 28, 1996. For her I accept your offer of psychiatric evaluation and litigation assistance services at $150.00 per hour plus expenses, and expert testimony at the rate of $200.00 per hour plus expenses. Travel time will be charged portal-to-portal. Your offer is accepted and a retainer of $1,000.00 is enclosed. I need your taxpayer identification number.

Kindly have your office contact me to arrange the child's visit at your facility. She will be accompanied by a relative and by me.

**Neither this letter, nor Dr. Morton's attached report, are discoverable by defendants.**

Dr. Edward Morton is a forensic psychologist. I interviewed him after his report. Because Monique's pre-existing cognitive deficits are so great, he is unwilling to establish a cause/effect link between Monique's scalding and disfigurement and her hyper-aggressiveness. In his opinion, the burns were only mildly disfiguring, easily covered, and no more stigmatizing than a birthmark. However, Dr. Morton suggested you might consider these issues:

- whether Monique's sincerely-held belief that she was scalded by foster parent Charles White has caused a victim-to-perpetrator syndrome. Among the numbered records, there is little documentation of her behavior prior to entering foster care. However, there are ample documents during foster care which describe Monique's outbursts. Comparing the pre-burn foster care behavior records with the post-burn school records, I observed that the former outbursts were principally directed at property, while the latter are directed at classmates. Drs. Morton said antagonistic instigation is Monique's play. I am told Monique is notorious for conflict in her neighborhood also.

- whether Monique has Post Traumatic Stress Disorder and, if so, to what extent was that condition caused or worsened by the burn, rather than by the havoc that led to foster care, and the foster care separation from her parent.

- whether the developmental testing pre-burn indicated a certain developmental curve which was not achieved or was delayed because of the burn, by comparing to the developmental testing post-burn. Or, maybe Monique was too close to the bottom to demonstrate a marked change.

You will form your own opinions based upon the thick bundle of numbered documents I have already discovered and as I may supplement, and upon your personal interviews and evaluation of Monique Meak. If you discern a condition which the burn caused or substantially contributed to, you will have to decide on a treatment plan. E.g., is psychotherapy viable given her deficits? What reasonable environmental changes might be called for? We have ready in New Orleans a psychiatric resident who can implement your plan.

To summarize, Monique Meak at age 4.5 years suffered first and second degree burns upon 10% of her body, including second degree burns on her buttocks, and deep second degree burns on her right leg, from contact with hot water in a bathroom tub while in a foster home. She had no burns to her hands or feet, and no splash marks. Determining Monique's future psychological effects and needs is complicated by pre-existing physical and psycho-social problems. Further, Monique has been judged incompetent to testify in deposition or at trial.

After reviewing this letter and the enclosed documents, Dr. Carney drew some tentative observations. She reserved her final conclusions until after she could hold two personal interviews with Monique.

- From a quantity of pain standpoint, Monique's type of burn causes the most. A four-year-old's skin is not thick like an adults'. Deep second burns meant daily debridement

- Much attention focused on her genitals.

- The course of treatment was even harder on Monique because her age and mental condition. The lack of close personal ties to her attendants created a limited ability to express the terror.

- This type of burn injury IS NOT a one-time trauma. The emotional changes are ingrained and will affect the quality of the rest of her life.

- The initial mental adjustment to scars is ugly self-image, that she is not desirable to others. In her youth she will probably hide the scars and withdraw from others for fear of rejection pain, or become aggressive with others. In her early teens she will probably reconcile that it is OK to live with scars. However, in her late teens she will encounter negative sorting which occurs during dating. This may develop into either a shyness leading to withdrawal, or into a thirst for affection. She will end up either closeted or more promiscuous. To find a husband will be more difficult.

- A burn such as hers can cause a pervading anxiety. Monique has some signs.

- If Monique sincerely believes someone else scalded her, this will cause anger, a feeling of helplessness, and a failure to trust. This will reinforce the not valuable feeling. This will spur the urge to fight back, to want to protect herself.

- Monique's key need will be a predictable environment with people who tolerate her. Talk therapy is recommended and it will have to be intensive and protracted due to the underlying cognitive deficits.

Frazier began making arrangements to get Monique seen by Dr. Carney. The first attempt, in the summer of 1999, fell through when Sarah Thompson refused to travel to Galveston. A second attempt was made in October 1999 to coincide with Dr. Carney's attendance at a New Orleans convention. This fell through because Frazier could not find a place to hold the interviews, and because OCS refused to deliver Monique.

Finally, in February 2000, Frazier was able to coordinate an overnight airplane trip to Dr. Carney in Galveston. Monique would be evaluated on April 10th and the 11th. Frazier had to agree to pay for an OCS social worker to escort Monique. Frazier also planned to bring his own daughter along to keep Monique company. Finally, just one day before the trip, Frazier was able to get a consent judgment from the Juvenile Court allowing him to take Monique to Galveston. That order read:

Considering plaintiff's Motion for Psychological Examination, the discussion held in chambers on February 10, 2000, and the consent of counsel below,

IT IS ORDERED: on April 10, 2000, DSS/OCS social worker Michelle Swift shall escort Monique Meak to Shriners Burn Hospital in Galveston, Texas for a 4:00 p.m. appointment with Dr. Wanda Carney, and again there at 10:00 a.m. on April 11, 2000. The escort will not attend these sessions. Round-trip airline travel between New Orleans and Houston Hobby, and overnight lodging in Galveston, are approved. All trip expenses for Monique Meak and her escort, except wages, are litigation advances payable by attorney Thomas Frazier.

# CHAPTER 19

In April 1999, Lana Meak asked again Frazier how she could regain custody of Monique. Talk to your own lawyer, he said. This time, Lana's Juvenile Court lawyer moved to modify Monique's disposition. Her motion was set for June 22nd. Frazier wrote Sarah Thompson, saying that Lana Meak has asked the Juvenile Court to take Monique from her. Frazier asked if he could visit Sarah and Monique. After two weeks Sarah called. She said she had moved to a new address and phone on St. Anthony Street in New Orleans. They talked about Lana's motion in Juvenile Court. Sarah told Frazier that Monique, while recently visiting with Lana, saw her mother attempt suicide by taking pills. Sarah promised to go to juvenile court and tell this to the judge. Also, Sarah needed Monique's school disciplinary file for a renewal of the child's SSI check. Frazier went to visit Monique at Sarah's new house. Everything appeared to be fine. He delivered to Sarah a copy of the school disciplinary file. When he got back to his office, Frazier forwarded Sarah and Monique's new address and phone number to all counsel.

By the beginning of May 1999 Frazier opposed Lana's Juvenile Court motion. He argued that Monique's best interest would be to keep the status quo, being sole custody in the paternal grandmother Sarah Thompson, and informal visitation by the mother Lana Meak with the consent of the custodian, and no OCS supervision. He argued that before custody could be returned to Lana Meak, she should first be ordered to produce her arrest records and her criminal disposition records, and that she also be ordered to comply with psychotherapy and substance abuse counseling.

By the time June 22nd had arrived, Lana was willing to take less than full custody. Frazier and Lana's lawyer entered a stipulation that granted Lana Meak regular overnight visitation at Lana's home. The Juvenile Court also ordered the Family Services Unit to conduct a home study of Lana Meak.

At the July 13 status hearing, the Juvenile Court judge ordered drug screens of Lana Meak and Demetrius Jackson. Frazier informed the judge that Monique and Sarah may have to travel to Galveston for a burn evaluation with Dr. Carney. By sidebar discussion, the judged directed OCS to look closely for domestic abuse between Lana Meak and her current man, and to determine child support from Demetrius Jackson.

In early August an OCS social worker told Frazier she might have to remove Monique from Sarah Thompson's home for hygienic reasons. The worker said Sarah was not bathing the child regularly, and that her hair was matted and uncombed. The complaint was made by a Family Services Unit worker. She said Monique could not be placed with Lana because Lana's home was not appropriate as she was having too many emotional battles with her current man. Frazier told the social worker that the father, Demetrius Jackson, was unsuitable too because he was only recently released from prison for armed robbery. He worked as busboy in a French Quarter restaurant, and he lived with his mother, Sarah Thompson. Frazier also said a Child Placement Services, Inc. foster home would not be appropriate because Monique was suing CPS. Frazier reminded the social worker to keep in mind that Monique has an IEP at school and that her hyperactivity-aggressiveness is well documented by the school.

Ten days later, at almost 10 p.m., Sarah Thompson called Frazier and said Monique was taken by ambulance to the New Orleans Adolescent Hospital. Monique was on a visit with her mother when Monique told Lana that she wanted to kill herself with a knife or by jumping out of a window. Sarah said NOAH had put the child on a 30-day hold. Sarah said Monique would not talk when Sarah visited. She said Lana accused her of allowing physical and sexual abuse to occur to Monique in Sarah's home. Sarah said Monique had no marks on her and was in good spirits when she left the night of

August 19th with Lana. Sarah said if any abuse occurred, it happened at Lana's.

The next day Frazier confirmed Monique was at NOAH. He tried to contact the OCS social workers but to no avail. He wrote the following emergency show cause motion and order:

Monique Meak was transported to New Orleans Adolescent Hospital for suicide ideation while on a visit with her mother. The child is scheduled to be released on September 9, 1999. The circumstances of her commitment and her needs following release ought to be reviewed before her release.

IT IS ORDERED that Lana Meak, Demetrius Jackson, and Sarah Thompson show cause at 3:30 p.m. on the 2nd day of September, 1999, why this Court should not enter any necessary order in the best interests of Monique

Meak. This may include orders affecting the custody and visitation rights of these parties, and/or orders which may return Monique Meak to the foster care custody of the State of Louisiana. Until that hearing is concluded, no one shall remove Monique Meak from her inpatient care at New Orleans Adolescent Hospital.

Frazier also contacted the tutors and the experts Dr. Morton and Dr. Carney.

Prior to the hearing, OCS obtained NOAH's records and shared them with Frazier. He summarized those records, serially numbered them, and shared them with all attorneys, Dr. Morton, Dr. Carney, and the tutors. Frazier wrote in his summary:

> NOAH's records recount that while on visit at her mother's home, Monique Meak threatened to jump out window or take pills. Monique said she wanted to kill herself and wanted to kill everybody. With her MD, Monique asked for a knife, but also denied wanting to kill herself. Told MD she wanted to

kill herself because she did not like her middle name.

According to Monique, her Uncle "Pete" touched her vagina with his penis, and Pete or a cousin hit her on the head. She told her grandmother Sarah, but was told to leave it alone. Said she wanted to kill herself because her uncle wanted to kill her and tried to make her eat grass and "dog poo poo." She described being offered "rock" but she threw it away.

Monique could not focus and she wandered from the topic several times. She was filled with anxiety due to mental retardation.

No history of suicidal or homicidal ideation, a spontaneous gesture. History of frequent temper tantrums, destroying furniture, cursing, bullying other children, poor impulse control, argumentative, not following rules. At school, history of frequently disruptive and disrespectful in Special Education class, fighting other children, refusing to do schoolwork, vulgar language.

Negative sexual abuse exam at University Hospital prior to NOAH admit. Full Scale IQ of 46 (moderately retarded). Overall reasoning lower than 99% of the children her age. Does not understand suicide, craves attention. Admitted to masturbating and touching female peers inappropriately. Typical behaviors during hospitalization included non-compliance, non-communicative, very hyperactive, opposition defiant, manipulative, and destructive when angry. Improvement noted while on Ritalin therapy, but violent outbursts led to time outs, therapeutic holds, and Benadryl injections. Accidentally injured herself (cut thumb) when she slammed a door.

Admitted as depressive disorder NOS, but revised to Impulse Control Disorder NOS, probable Post Traumatic Stress Disorder, ADHD, moderate mental retardation. Difficult to assess abuse because Monique is mentally retarded and possibly has pervasive levels disorder. Bed wetting.

Outpatient care at Chartres Mental Health Clinic (Ritalin 5 mg x 3 daily). Per social worker: setting firm limits for Monique and constant adherence, address her use of manipulative behaviors, needs close supervision in Sarah Thompson's household, and supervised visitation with Lana Meak's household. Per psychologist: strongly recommends referral to OCDD. Prescription glasses. Assist with school placement. Per treatment team: dysfunctional home life likely to interfere with treatment, prognosis poor if patient remains in current home situation. Per MD: needs outpatient services from mental health clinic, mental rehab services, "Pt. needs a structured environment for safety." Discharged to live with aunt Ronnie Thompson, who lives next door to grandmother Sarah.

Diagnosis:
AXIS I:    Attention deficit disorder

|         |                                 |
|---------|---------------------------------|
|         | Impulse control disorder        |
| AXIS II: | Moderate Mental Retardation    |
| AXIS III: | History of fetal alcohol syndrome |
| AXIS IV: | Problems with support group    |
| AXIS V: | GAF 58                          |

At the next hearing, the OCS attorney said she will argue Monique needs structured custody, perhaps community placement.

Little was accomplished at the September 2nd hearing. It was stipulated that Monique would remain with her aunt Ronnie Thompson pending further orders. No medical witness answered the subpoena, and there was a due process problem with Lana Meak making accusations against Sarah Thompson and Demetrius Jackson when the grandmother and father did not have their own attorneys. The case was continued until October 28th.

Monique's aunt Ronnie Thompson lived next door to Sarah Thompson and Demetrius Jackson. This did not please Lana Meak. She called Frazier to complain, but her referred her to her own attorney. Counsel for OCS said it had hired a social worker to intensively shadow Monique in order to prepare a comprehensive report. Frazier shared a copy of the 1,600+ pages he had assembled so far in the burn case. The social worker told Frazier that Monique was currently suspended from school for 5 days for fighting.

Monique had barely returned to school when, on October 14th, OCS removed her from school and placed her in foster care in a group home. The reason was a validated finding of sexual abuse. The next day the Juvenile Court issued a new hold order.

Frazier wrote and filed the following motions at Juvenile Court:

## MOTION FOR MEDICAL EXAMINATION

Monique Meak has the right to move for her own medical examination, Ch.C. art. 867(A). On the child's behalf, her counsel requests a lock of her hair be removed and sampled for narcotics exposure. Good cause for this testing exists in the attached NOAH records which attribute this statement to her, "I do drugs with my uncle. Rock. He gives me rock I throw it away."

Should the hair sampling prove negative exposure to illicit drugs, that finding will have a bearing on the child's credibility. Should the hair sample be positive for drug exposure, the child reserves the right to demand hair sampling of all residents of any familial household seeking her custody. See "appropriateness," Ch.C. art. 675(B)(1), and "conditions", Ch.C. art. 681(A)(1).

Mover prays this sampling be done immediately and at the State's cost (the child is indigent and resides in State's custody) and that the results be made known to the court and all counsel within 30 days, Ch.C. art. 867.

## MOTION FOR COMPETENCY HEARING

At a continued custody hearing, reasonable grounds were found to believe that Monique Meak may be a sexually abused child in need of care, and that separation from family was necessary for her safety and protection. Yet, the same hearing also revealed that the sole informant is Monique Meak, an eight-year-old child with a 46 I.Q., and with numerous social adjustment problems. Monique Meak has a history of disruptive behavior in her special education classes and in home settings. Her mental capacity and behavior raise a question of her credibility.

The District Attorney has offered no evidence of harm to confirm the alleged sexual abuse. OCS's abuse screener, Dr. Scott Broussard, found her sexual exam to be in normal limits. Nor did the District Attorney offer any evidence of mental harm linked to the alleged abuse. Psychiatrist Dr. Stephen Cornish, who treated the child for 19 days at NOAH just one month ago, did not make a cause-effect link between the alleged abuse and the hospitalization. In fact, Dr. Cornish found it difficult to assess the child's abuse allegations because of her mental retardation and probable pervasive levels disorder. Dr. Cornish's diagnosis did not cite sexual abuse. This lack of evidence of physical or mental harm goes to the "seriously endanger" clause in Ch.C. art. 603(1) and also infers a question of the child's credibility.

It would be an error at the adjudication to admit Monique Meak's out-of-court statements without first testing her competency. See C.Evid. art. 601. Incompetence may not bar admissibility of those out-of-court allegations, but it will have a strong bearing on weight.

While this Court is not bound by the decisions of the Civil District Court, it would seem likely that this Court will find Monique Meak incompetent as she has already been declared incompetent to depose or testify in her tort action for the foster home scalding.

Without a competency hearing, this impaired child's uncorroborated allegations pose a real danger of an unwarranted liberty restriction.

Accordingly, child's counsel moves for a competency exam to be conducted privately, with a record, and with only counsel in attendance. Mover offers these questions:

1. How old are you?

2. In what year were you born?

3. Where does your father live?

4. What is your father's name?

5. What does your father do for a living?

6. Where does your mother live?

7. What is your mother's name?

8. What does your mother do for a living?

9. Where does your grandmother Sarah live?

10. What does she do for a living?

11. Where does your grandmother Rose live?

12. What does she do for a living?

13. Why were you living with your aunt Ronnie Thompson?

14. How do you help at home?

15. How many brothers and sisters do you have?

16. How old are they?

17. What is the name of your school?

18. What time do you go to school?

19. What time do you come home from school?

20. What subjects do you take at school?

21. Who takes you to school?

22. What is your favorite color?

23. What is your favorite TV show?

24. I told you my name when we started. What is my name?

25. Do you know what the truth is?

26. Is it bad to say something that is not true?

27. If I ask you to always tell me the truth, will you do it?

28. What color is my robe?

29. Suppose I tell you that my black robe is (another color). Now tell me, what color is my robe?

All counsel should be permitted to file additional questions. Any objection to the exam or decision shall be made on the record after Monique Meak is removed from chambers.

## MOTION FOR VIDEOTAPE TESTIMONY

If the Court determines Monique Meak is competent, and if all parties do not waive trial testimony from her, then child's counsel moves for her testimony to be preserved through a prehearing videotape, Ch.C. art. 326-327.

## MOTION FOR INFORMAL ADJUSTMENT

Alternatively, if the Court determines Monique Meak incompetent, then child's counsel moves the Court to void any adjudication petition based solely her out of court statements, to modify the prior disposition of non-parental family custody, and either to order the parties to prepare an informal adjustment agreement which changes the case plan to FINS, Ch.C. art. 628.

## MOTION TO SEE DR. CARNEY

Monique Meak has pending in the Civil District Court a suit for damages arising out of the January 1996 scalding in a foster home bathtub. She desires to be personally seen by her expert, burn psychologist Dr. Wanda Carney at Shriner's Burn Hospital in Galveston, Texas. Monique Meak is without funds to pay Dr. Carney for her work, and is without funds to travel to Galveston. Therefore, the child moves the Court for an order requiring OCS to pay the expenses of the consultation and travel, and to provide her with an escort for an overnight stay in Texas.

The October 28th hearing opened with a bang. The DA filed a surprise motion to disqualify Frazier from representing Monique due to the mistaken idea of a conflict of interest. The DA thought Frazier represented grandmother Sarah Thompson. Frazier explained to the DA that he never represented Sarah Thompson in any court, and that he only represented Monique in Juvenile Court and her duly confirmed tutrix in the Civil District Court. The motion to disqualify was withdrawn.

Next, the judge took up the rest of the motions. She ordered the DA to file a petition by November 12th, with answers due at the November 22nd trial. The previous order for psychiatric and psychological evaluations was dissolved; but neurological and physical exams will be done without the presence of any counsel. Motion to consolidate the new case with the old case was granted. OCS testified that Monique is placed at Bethlehem Children's Home where she had continued behavior problems. The group home was trying to make her docile by upping the Ritalin, or maybe by giving her something else. No one had visited. Frazier may attend a November 10th team meeting. OCS will find name of the person at Bethlehem to whom Monique repeated the sexual abuse allegations. OCS will look into getting glasses for her. Although now schooled at Morial Elementary, Monique's new IEP will place her in Bethlehem's school in early November.

Motion for Medical Examination (hair) was denied without reasons. Motion for Competency Hearing was granted after Frazier clarified that he feared Monique might be adjudicated solely as a result of her low intelligence and not because something wrong was actually done to her. OCS will bring Monique to court on November 22nd. All of the remaining motions were tabled pending the competency hearing except the Dr. Carney motion was denied without reasons. During a sidebar, Frazier stated that he had acted ethically under the rules regarding a client under disability.

On November 10th, Frazier travelled to the Bethlehem group home for the team planning meeting. Dr. Chevareaux was in charge. Frazier provided him with copies of the NOAH psychological assessment and discharge summary. The low dose of Ritalin was not calming Monique. Dr. Chevareaux will try an increase from 7.5 x 3 to 10 x 3. If this doesn't work, Dr. Chevareaux will switch to a newer anti-psychotic. The doctor is alert to increased potential for pharmaceutical side effects. A neurologic assessment is underway; CT or MRI will be performed. The doctor does not need hair analysis to treat Monique. Because Monique was congenitally damaged, raised badly, with suicidal ideation, and hyper-sexual, she is now under 24-hour visual watch. Her school must guarantee the same vigilance, say in a three-child class, or she will be schooled at Bethlehem. The treatment goal is to make Monique happy and docile so she can be cared for. If she is not successful at Bethlehem, the next recommendation will be confinement in a locked residential facility. Dr. Chevareaux does not think anyone in family will be able to raise Monique.

The adjudication petition was served at court. The judge dismissed Monique's parents, holding that the only party who could be sued was grandmother Sarah Thompson, Monique's former legal custodian. Sarah Thompson denied the neglect and abuse allegations. The hearing was then adjourned to wait for Monique's arrival. When she finally was brought to court the competency hearing began. The judge asked the questions and Monique responded. There were no objections. Monique was judged competent. Trial was set for December 9th.

At trial, Sarah Thompson stipulated that Monique at present was a child in need of care without admitting to the petition's allegations about the past. She gave up the right to be a relative placement, yet requested visitation rights. A reunification plan was crafted which, among other things, required Lana Meak to attend programs designated by OCS.

Two months later, Frazier drafted and filed a motion for subpoenas:

> Child's counsel respectfully represents: On December 9, 1999, Monique Meak was adjudicated a child in need of care. She has been made to live in a very restrictive placement, an intensive care residential group home. The reunification plan requires "the mother .... to

attend any and all programs the Agency arranges in working toward reunification." The judgment is vague about program content because OCS did not have any specifics ready for the December 9 hearing.

Defining the training and resources needed to transition this child to a lesser restrictive family-type placement is an important substantive due process issue. Monique Meak requests two subpoenas issue for the March 13, 2000 review:

1. To define need, testimony from Monique Meak's residential social worker is required.

2. To match to resources (per Ch.C. art. 672), testimony is required from the DSS designee most knowledgeable about the scope of resources available.

Not much was accomplished at the next hearing because the subpoena to Bethlehem failed. It was reissued for June. OCS said it was putting the case on a dual track: an unlikely reunification with the mother, or a possible relative placement with a cousin who is a Texas social worker named Lisa Grande.

Frazier wrote Ms. Grande about her interest in Monique but received no reply. Three days later Frazier drove to Bethlehem and visited Monique's social worker. They talked about the upcoming court appearance and Monique's April 10th trip to Galveston. A few days after that trip, Frazier again visited with Monique and her grandmother Sarah at Bethlehem.

# CHAPTER 20

In the meantime, while Monique's Juvenile Court case raged, Frazier conducted legal research into amending the scalding petition with claims for a civil rights violation. A civil rights action comes from a federal law, 42 U.S.C.A. § 1983. That law states:

> Every person who, under color of any statute, ordinance, regulation, custom or usage, of any State or Territory or the District of Columbia, subjects, or causes to be subjected, any citizen of the United States or other person within the jurisdiction thereof to the deprivation of any rights, privileges, or immunities secured by the Constitution and laws shall be liable to the party injured in an action at law, suit in equity, or other proper proceeding for redress.

Frazier outlined his legal research. A state. its agencies and political subdivisions are not persons within the meaning of § 1983. Will v. Michigan Department of State Police, 491 U.S. 58, 70-72, 109 S.Ct. 2304, 2312, 105 L.Ed.2d 45 (1989). However, state officers may be held liable in their personal, but not official, capacity. Ex Parte Young, 209 U.S. 123, 28

S.Ct. 441, 52 L.Ed. 714 (1908). Private citizens are not immune. Wyatt v. Cole, 504 U.S. 158, 112 S.Ct. 1827, 118 L.Ed.2d 504 (1992).

In order to prevail in a § 1983 civil rights action, the plaintiffs must prove by a preponderance of the evidence that the conduct of the defendants was under the color of state law and that the conduct resulted in a deprivation of rights, privileges, and immunities secured by the United States Constitution or a federal statute, or both. Parratt v. Taylor, 451 U.S. 527, 101 S.Ct. 1908, 68 L.Ed.2d 420 (1981); Moresi v. State, Department of Wildlife and Fisheries, 567 So.2d 1081, 1084 (La. 1990). The violation does not have to be willful. Monroe v. Pape, 365 U.S. 167 (1961).

Foster children have a due process right to be free from the infliction of unnecessary harm. McComb v. Wambaugh, 934 F.2d 474 (C.A. 3 1991); K.H. through Murphy v. Morgan, 914 F.2d 846 (7th Cir. 1990); Meador v. Cabinet for Human Resources, 902 F.2d 474 (6th Cir.), cert. den., 111 S.Ct. 182

(1990); Milburn by Milburn v. Anne Arundel County Dept. of Social Services, 871 F.2d 474 (C.A. 4 1989), reh. den., cert. den., 110 S.Ct. 148; and Taylor by and through Walker v. Ledbetter, 818 F.2d 791 (C.A. 11 1987), cert. den. 109 S.Ct. 1337.

A § 1983 plaintiff may be awarded compensatory damages for special losses such as medical expenses, general damages for physical and mental pain and suffering, and punitive damages. Memphis Community School District v. Stachura, 477 U.S. 299, 306, 106 S.Ct. 2537, 2542-43, 91 L.Ed.2d 249 (1986). Attorney's fees and costs are recoverable under 42 U.S.C. § 1988 if plaintiff shows that the defendant's conduct was either motivated by evil motive or intent, or showed reckless or callous indifference to the rights of others. Smith v. Wade, 461 U.S. 30, 56, 103 S.Ct. 1625, 1640, 75 L.Ed.2d 632 (1983). Punitive damages are available in § 1983 actions filed in Louisiana state courts, Booze v. City of Alexandria, 94-0763 (La. 4/4/94), 637 So.2d 91, 92.

The Johnson v. Georgia Highway Express, Inc., 488 F.2d 714, 717-19 (5th Cir. 1974) decision established twelve factors to determine how much attorney fees should be awarded:

(1) the time and labor required;

(2) the novelty and difficulty of the questions:

(3) the skill requisite to perform the legal service properly;

(4) the preclusion of other employment by the attorney due to acceptance of the case;

(5) the customary fee;

(6) whether the fee is fixed or contingent;

(7) time limitations imposed by the client or the circumstances;

(8) the amount involved and the results obtained:

(9) the experience, reputation, and ability of the attorneys;

(10)  the "undesirability" of the case;

(11) the nature and length of the professional relationship with the client; and

(12) awards in similar cases.

Additionally, a prevailing plaintiff may recover all reasonable out-of-pocket expenses normally charged to a fee-paying client. Associated Builders & Contractors of Louisiana, Inc. v. Orleans Parish School Board, 919 F.2d 374, 380 (5th Cir. 1990).

Frazier advised the tutors that a § 1983 action should be filed. The proof would be hardly greater than the tort case. Perhaps more money would result from punitive damages and attorney fees. Just filing the action would create settlement leverage. The tutors agreed, so Frazier filed it in October 1999.

## SECOND AMENDED PETITION

The minor Monique Meak, through undersigned counsel, reasserts all prior allegations not modified below.

The petition is **amended** by adding new paragraph 12:

12.

Department of Social Services, as fiduciary to Monique Meak, is solidarily liable for all damages owed by Barbara White, Charles White, and Child Placement Services, Inc.

The petition is **amended** by new paragraphs 13-19 within this court's concurrent jurisdiction.

FIRST CIVIL RIGHTS CAUSE OF ACTION

13.

Charles White acted under color of state law because:

a) he was a foster parent agent of the state.

b) foster parentage is a legal relation serving an exclusively governmental function, and having

Charles White supply it was exclusively the prerogative of the state.

c) a symbiotic relationship existed whereby Charles White discharged the state's child-rearing obligation to its ward. and/or

d) his foster parentage was state encouraged or facilitated.

14.

Monique Meak was deprived of her liberty and right to be free from damage to her bodily integrity when Charles White, by deliberate indifference or more culpably, immersed her into scalding water and caused her damages, all in violation of 42 U.S.C. § 1983 and the due process clause of the Fourteenth Amendment to the United States Constitution, entitling her tutrix to recover compensatory damages, punitive damages and attorney's fees and expenses.

15.

The absence of splash marks, and the absence of burns on the extremities, indicates a non-accidental scalding by dipping or immersion. State v. Sepulvado, 93-2692 (La. 4/8/96); 672 So.2d 158.

SECOND CIVIL RIGHTS CAUSE OF ACTION

16.

Child Placement Services, Inc. acted under color of state law by one or more reasons:

a) it was an agent of the state;

b) a symbiotic relationship existed between it and the state to discharge the state's child-rearing duty; and/or

c) its services were encouraged or facilitated by the state.

17.

Before Monique Meak was put in the White foster home, Child Placement Services, Inc. several times certified the home for safety with a state-provided checklist including:

**The hot water accessible to the children does not exceed 120 degrees Fahrenheit at the outlet. (This does not apply to faucets that can mix hot and cold water.)**

With deliberate indifference or more culpability, Child Placement Services, Inc. violated federal substantive due process protections by (1) never putting a thermometer into the hot-only water flow at the Whites' bathroom tub to determine if the temperature exceeded 120 degrees Fahrenheit; (2) failing to inform the state that the hot water had not been tested thereby withholding from the state information essential to Monique Meak's protection; (3) failure to ensure that the White home was free of unsafe scalding hazards;

(4) failing to uncover and correct a foreseeable scald hazard to foster children such as Monique Meak; (5) never installing automatic temperature or flow regulators in the White home; and (6) never requiring the Whites to install automatic temperature or flow regulators. Child Placement Services, Inc. offered the White home to the state for Monique's placement, notwithstanding the scalding water hazard.

18.

Monique Meak was deprived of her liberty and right to be free from state-occasioned damage to her bodily integrity when Child Placement Services, Inc., by deliberate indifference or more culpably, interpreted and implemented the state's home inspection criteria to permit the White foster home tub to deliver scalding water, then offering that unsafe home for her placement, all a "but for" or "substantial factor" cause of Monique Meak's damages. This violated 42 U.S.C. § 1983 and the due process clause of the Fourteenth Amendment to the United States Constitution, entitling her tutrix to recover compensatory damages, punitive damages, attorney's fees and expenses.

19.

Should the Department of Social Services assert a R.S. 13:5106 foster care lien to limit or offset its liability in any way, then plaintiff seeks a declaration that R.S. 13:5106 is unconstitutional by (a) the Louisiana Constitution's waiver of sovereign immunity, or by (b) the Supremacy Clause of the United States Constitution.

The prayer is **amended** in the following respects:

WHEREFORE, Monique Meak's tutrix prays that, on the state law causes of action, that there be judgment against the defendants, Barbara White, wife of/and Charles White, Allstate Insurance Co., Child Placement Services, Inc., Scottsdale Insurance Co., and the Department of Social Services, holding them severally, jointly and in solido liable for compensatory damages reasonable in the premises, together with court costs in this action and the court costs in Monique Meak's tutorship action, legal interest from the date of judicial demand, and all other general and equitable relief, including a declaration that R.S. 13:5106 is unconstitutional if asserted.

Further, Monique Meak's tutrix prays that, on the federal law causes of action, that there be judgment against the defendants, Charles White, Allstate Insurance Co., Child Protection Services,

Inc., and Scottsdale Insurance Co., holding them severally, jointly and in solido liable for compensatory damages reasonable in the premises, for punitive damages, for attorney's fees and expenses, together with court costs in this action and the court costs of Monique Meak's tutorship action, legal interest from the date of judicial demand, and all other general and equitable relief.

Further, Monique Meak's tutrix prays that, on the fiduciary liability cause of action, that there be judgment against the defendant, Department of Social Services, holding it solidarily liable for all sums owed by Barbara White, Charles White, and Child Placement Services., Inc.

This amended petition was served on all the defendants in late October and early November 1999. On November 22nd,

Allstate removed the case to federal court. Moreover, Allstate's answer pleaded that the tutrix was liable for Monique's damages. Frazier discussed these developments with the tutors, and it was decided that Frazier should research, prepare and file a motion to remand and a motion for Rule 11 sanctions:

## MOTION FOR REMAND

Plaintiff urges remand due to many defects.

## FACTS

This cause arose when a 4 ½-year-old girl, Monique Meak, was scalded in a foster home. She is represented by her court-appointed tutrix. Suit was filed in state court on January 28, 1997.

The defendants are the foster parents, Barbara White and Charles White; their homeowner's insurer, Allstate Insurance Co.; the foster home placement agency Child Placement Services, Inc. and its insurer Scottsdale Ins. Co.;

and the Louisiana Department of Social Services. The state Department of Health and Hospitals intervened for its medical lien, and is not a "defendant" for removal and remand purposes.

The first time a federal cause of action was pleaded was the Second Amended Petition filed October 4, 1999. It was first served upon defendant Child Placement Services, Inc. on October 20, 1999. See attached proof of service from the Civil Sheriff, Parish of Orleans.

On November 22, 1999, Allstate Insurance Co. filed a notice of removal ("Petition for Removal") bearing only the signature of Allstate's counsel. That notice says "Defendants, Allstate Insurance Company, Child Placement Services Corporation [sic], Scottsdale Insurance Company, and the State of Louisiana, Department of Social Services, consent to the removal of the case."

LAW

When a federal question is first asserted in an amended petition, the deadline to notice the case's removal is 30 days from the date the amended petition was first served on any defendant. 28 U.S.C. § 1446(b). If the first defendant served does not seek removal within 30 days, his right to remove is waived. That waiver means the other defendants cannot remove the case because the first defendant cannot consent to removal. Brooks v. Rosiere, 585 F.Supp. 351, 352 (E.D. La. 1984).

Generally, all defendants must unanimously join in the removal. Each defendant must timely file a notice of removal or a writing indicating consent to the removal sought by another. Doe v. Kerwood, 969 F.2d 165, 167-168

(5th Cir. 1992); Brooks v. Rosiere, supra at 383.

This writing requirement is not satisfied by one

defendant's mere allegation that the others do not

object, Roe v. O'Donohue, 38 F.3d 298, 301 (7th

Cir. 1994); Ogletree v. Barnes, 851 F.Supp. 184,

188-189 (E.D. Pa. 1994); Miles v. Kilgore, 928

F.Supp. 1071, 1077-78 (N.D. Ala. 1996).

Further, a notice of removal is defective if

it fails to adequately explain why any served

defendant failed to join in the notice of removal.

Home Owners Funding Corp. of Am. v. Allison,

756 F.Supp. 290, 291-292 (N.D. Tex. 1991); P.P.

Farmer's Elevator Co. v. Farmers Elevator Mut.

Ins. Co., 395 F.2d 546, 548 (7th Cir. 1969).

ANALYSIS

Because the Second Amended Petition was

first served on October 20, 1999, then the 30th

day deadline to remove was Friday, November 19, 1999. Allstate's November 22, 1999 notice was untimely.

Further, there is no proof of unanimity among the defendants. Only one defendant of five has complied with the written notice requirement. Allstate's allegation of consent is defective by lack of a writing signed by each joining defendant.

Last, Allstate's notice is defective fails to adequately explain the silence of its own insureds, Barbara White and Charles White. They have separate counsel, are central parties to the case, and were served with the amended petition.

Allstate's improvident removal ought to trigger reasonable attorney's fees and expenses.

## MOTION FOR RULE 11 SANCTIONS

Even if the case is remanded, this Rule still lies in the Court's collateral jurisdiction.

Plaintiff's counsel certifies that, on November 23, 1999, he personally discussed this matter with counsel for the defendant, Allstate Insurance Co., to no avail.

THE PLEADING AT ISSUE

Allstate's Answer, filed in federal court on November 22, 1999, states:

"FIFTH DEFENSE

At all times relevant herein the cause of this incident was the fault and negligence of Alberta Jones, Esq. the dative tutrix ad litem of Monique Meak in the following particulars:

(a)    Failure to properly and completely inform Barbara White and Charles White of the physical, mental and emotional limitations of Monique Meak;

(b)    Failure to properly and completely inform the State of Louisiana, Department of Social Services of the physical, mental and emotional limitations of Monique Meak;

(c)    Failure to properly and completely inform Child Placement Services, Inc. of the physical, mental and emotional limitations of Monique Meak;

(d)    Failure to ensure that Barbara White and Charles White fully understood and appreciated the physical, mental and emotional conditions and limitations of Monique Meak;

(e)    Any and all other acts of negligence to be proved at time of trial on the merits."

## LAW

Rule 11 sanctions apply if a joinder is baseless or lacks plausibility. Community Electric Service of Los Angeles, Inc. v. National

Elec. Contractors Ass'n, Inc., 869 F.2d 1235 (9th Cir. 1989), cert. den. 493 U.S. 891, 110 S.Ct. 236, 107 L.Ed.2d 187. A party is not obliged to update his pleadings, but each subsequent pleading must satisfy Rule 11 according to facts known at the time of signing. Curley v. Brignoli, Curley & Roberts, Associates, 123 F.R.D. 613 (S.D.N.Y. 1989), cert. den. 111 S.Ct. 1430, 113, L.Ed.2d 484. After learning that an assistant superintendent did not begin working at a prison until nine months after the beating incidents, and after discovering no evidence that he participated in any cover-up of the beatings, then Rule 11 sanctions were appropriate when plaintiff continued to name the assistant superintendent as a defendant. Denny v. Hinton, 131 F.R.D. 659 (M.D.N.C. 1990), aff'd, 937 F.2d 602 (4th Cir. 1991).

## FACTS

Foster child Monique Meak was scalded on January 28, 1996. Nearly eight months later attorney Alberta Jones, Esq. was appointed as the child's litigation representative. Those orders were specially pleaded May 31, 1997 in Plaintiff's First Supplemental and Amended Petition. The same orders were shared with Allstate in discovery. Yet, Allstate's answer denied her appointment and alleged the tutrix Jones to be at fault.

Allstate has no factual basis for this allegation. It is highly unlikely that two courts sitting in tutorship, the Orleans Parish Juvenile Court and the Orleans Parish Civil District Court, would appoint a tortfeasor as tutrix. But sanctions are not sought for the initial pleading in state court. It is the federal court pleading, made after three years of discovery, against which sanctions are sought. Allstate has received copies of Jones' appointment orders. Further, Allstate has received more than a sixteen hundred pages of other documents, and Allstate has participated in at least a half-dozen depositions. Nowhere has there been uncovered the least sniff any connection between Monique Meak at the time of the scalding, and her future dative tutrix ad litem.

Allstate knew it should not allege tutrix fault when the tutrix and the child were strangers until nine months after the scalding. Now, in federal court, after years of deep discovery, Allstate has repeated its baseless allegation. No one else has alleged tutrix fault.

WHEREFORE Alberta Jones, Esq., as the dative tutrix ad litem of Monique Meak, prays these Rule 11 sanctions be ordered against

Allstate Insurance Co.: (a) to strike all allegations and prayers that Alberta Jones, Esq. was at fault for the scalding of Monique Meak, and (b) to pay the undersigned counsel a reasonable sum for attorney's fees and costs.

The federal judge granted the motion to remand in January 2000. The case was ordered returned to the Civil District Court. The federal judge also granted the Rule 11 sanctions striking Allstate's pleadings against the tutrix.

Instead of itemizing his hours and costs, Frazier demanded Allstate settle the whole case by paying its medical payments coverage of $5,000 and paying $5,000 of its liability coverage, reserving all rights against Barbara White and Charles White. Allstate refused, saying it could not settle without the full release of its insureds. Frazier replied that the only way he could dismiss the Whites would be if DSS stipulated it was liable for the fault of the Whites as if they were still parties.

# CHAPTER 21

While Monique's case was moving along in the Juvenile Court, and while the civil rights actions were pleaded in the Civil District Court, and while remand was being fought in federal court, Frazier was also busy hunting down a plumbing expert to testify about the scalding hazard in the White home. He decided that the best expert would be a free representative of the state Plumbing Board. Frazier noticed the deposition of a plumbing board representative.

Next, Frazier made lengthy searches of legal materials and Internet sources to prepare a fact sheet about scalding:

> I work for Monique Meak, a little girl who was scalded in the bathtub of a residential foster home. She was 4 years old. The scald covered 10% of her body and put her in the hospital for 19 days. She has permanent scars on her buttocks and right thigh, and emotional problems.

> The defendants are foster parents Barbara White and Charles White of New Orleans East, the foster care contractor Child Placement Services, Inc., and the Louisiana Department of Social Services. I am seeking expert testimony about:

- the hazard of hot water scalding
- anti-scald devices available before January 1996
- how they work to give reliable, passive protection
- capability for residential installation
- cost

No code requires anti-scald devices in residential homes. But when that private residence is a foster home, the Louisiana Administrative Code specifies:

1. Foster home bathroom must have an adequate supply of hot and cold running water, L.A.C. 48:I.6133(A) and L.A.C. 48:I.6139(E).

2. The home shall be free of hazards to the family health, L.A.C. 48:I.6139(A).

Furthermore, when the foster homes are inspected, the state requires:

**The hot water accessible to the children does not exceed 120 degrees Fahrenheit at the outlet. (This does not apply to faucets that can mix hot and cold water.)**

Types of anti-scald devices:

**1. <u>temperature actuated flow reduction valve</u>** will not resume flow until faucets are reset. Cost ranges from $18.99 to $30.00, no plumber required.

**2. thermostatic mixing valves** one per hot water heater, Cost ranges from $74.95 - $109.80, plumber required.

**3. pressure compensating mixing valves** resist thermal shock due to pressure fluctuations, but not truly anti-scald as will deliver full hot on demand regardless of tank temperature. Cost $69.95, plumber required.

**4. thermostatic and pressure compensating mixing valves** like #3, but will not deliver full hot.

Other scald prevention measures:

REDUCE WATER HEATER TEMPERATURE
Usually installed at 140 - 150 degrees. However, thermostats are often unreliable. A hot water heater set at 120 degrees is not ideal for dishwashing and laundry purposes, may result in insufficient hot water for high demand periods, and may allow Legionella pneumophilia bacteria (Legionnaire's disease) to grow in tank.

"CHILD-PROOF" FAUCET VALVES
If building or remodeling, move faucets to 36" to 40" above tub floor. Otherwise, install "push & turn" type valve handles (like medicine bottles).

BATHING PRECAUTIONS
Draw cold water first, then add hot water to the bath, then test temperature by hand. Use

cheap in-tub liquid crystal bath thermometer.
Maintain continuous supervision of child in tub.

The attorney for DSS agreed to furnish a representative of the

Plumbing Board at a date, time and place mutually convenient

to all counsel. Frazier forwarded a copy of the fact sheet to

DSS counsel, saying he would use it in the deposition.

# CHAPTER 22

After the scalding case returned to Civil District Court from federal court, a new pre-trial conference was held on February 10, 2000. New trial dates were picked. The first day of trial would be October 23rd. A new pre-trial order was issued establishing cut-off dates.

During the conference, Judge Gardner floated the possibility of a $100,000 settlement, and questioned Frazier's demand of $125,000. She encouraged the parties to mediate, but Frazier said mediation would have to wait until Dr. Carney could issue her report and be deposed.

## Timetable

| | |
|---|---|
| Apr. 10 | first exam by Dr. Carney in Galveston |
| Apr. 11 | second exam by Dr. Carney in Galveston |
| May | depose Dr. Carney (date not fixed) |
| May | depose Plumbing Board (date not fixed) |
| **May** | **MEDIATION (DATE NOT FIXED)** |
| Aug. 1 | plaintiff and defendant witness lists due |
| Aug. 15 | last day to issue interrogatories |
| Sept. 1 | discovery cut-off |
| Sept. 11 | last day to file motions, exceptions, and summary judgments |
| **Sept. 23** | **LAST DAY FOR NUDE PHOTOS** |

| | |
|---|---|
| Sept. 23 | trial subpoena cut-off |
| Sept. 23 | last day to post jury bond |
| Oct. 6 | last day to hear motions, exceptions, and summary judgments |
| Oct. 9 | stipulations and exhibits conference, before Oct. 20 |
| Oct. 9 | serve proposed jury instructions and interrogatories |
| Oct. 16 | meet & file joint jury I&I, and any I&I not jointly proposed |
| Oct. 20 | last day to make jury bond deposit ($240 x 4 days) |
| Oct. 21 | object to opponent's I&I |
| Oct. 23 | have may call list ready for jurors |
| Oct. 23 | reply brief to any objections to own I&I |
| Oct. 23 | offer voir dire questions for Court, have 15 minutes of own |
| **Oct. 23** | **8:30 TRIAL (FIRST DAY OF FOUR)** |

Frazier received from Tulane Hospital a copy of Monique's neurological work-up and MRIs. He serially stamped these documents and forwarded copies to each of the attorneys and experts. He did the same with records received from Bethlehem Children's Home and with photos from the Galveston trip. When he received Dr. Carney's report on July 17th, he also forwarded it to all attorneys and interested parties at the Juvenile Court.

Dr. Carney's report summarized the documents she had been sent, and chronicled Monique's evaluations. Unfortunately, during the Galveston interviews, the child failed to open up and talk about her injuries. On the last page of her report, Dr. Carney recommended:

1. **Placement in a stable family environment with care-taking assistance provided to the parent(s) of the family to prevent their exhaustion.**

2. **Family therapy/counseling provided by an expert.**

3. **Individual psychotherapy and psychiatric treatment for Monique with the goals of overcoming the effects of trauma and developing a positive body image and a positive self-regard.**

4. **A special education program that emphasizes socialization as well as academics and job training.**

Frazier forwarded this recommendation to an expert economist to price their cost. That expert's report returned in a week, showing a cost in excess of $250,000.

In the meantime, the Juvenile Court case continued. A June 6th status conference was continued until June 26th because Lana had given birth to a new baby. On June 26th it was stipulated that OCS would retain custody of Monique and keep her at Bethlehem, that the plan had changed to termination of parental rights by consent with the goal of an adoption by the Texas cousin. Grandmother Sarah Thompson retained her visitation rights. At the next hearing, July 12th, it was announced that Demetrius Jackson had surrendered his parental rights, but that Lana Meak had not. OCS was to file a Termination of Parental Rights suit against Lana before the end of August.

Frazier drafted and filed a timely witness list in the scalding suit:

## PLAINTIFF'S WITNESS LIST

1. Martha Whorley, Section Administrator of the Policy Section, La. DSS.

2. Priscilla Bruce, Joyce Allen and Darlene Jones, designees of La. DSS/OCS.

3. Designee of the Louisiana State Plumbing Board most familiar with anti-scald devices.

4. Laura Jetson, Gilda Franklin and Sonia Smith, designees of Child Placement Services, Inc.

5. Barbara White

6. Charles White, Sr.

7. Dr. William Larson, Jr.

8. Dr. Scott A. Broussard

9. Mrs. Sarah Thompson

10. Michelle Swift, La. DSS/OCS.

11. Tammy Johnson, Bethlehem Children's Treatment Center, Inc.

12. Dr. Wanda Carney, Shriner's Burn Hospital, Galveston

13. Dr. Marlon Lyon, Forensic Economics Corp.

14. T. Alberta Jones, Esq., tutrix

15. Michael Harmon, Esq., undertutor

16. Any witness needed to identify or authenticate any exhibit not stipulated admissible.

17. Any witness listed by any other party

For some unknown reason, not one of the defense attorneys filed a timely witness list. When he discovered his omission, the first thing Skinner Auld did was call Frazier and whine. Auld begged him to let him file a late list. Frazier was in no mood to compromise, and told Auld so. Auld faxed over a long nagging letter. So Frazier decided to reply in kind. He wrote this letter and copied it to all counsel:

Dear Skinner,

I have yours of August 2. Since you've decided to write up your side of an hour-long conversation, and to tack on new grievances, then I'll address you in kind.

Bottom line: I'm not bailing out any lawyer who blew their August 1st deadline for witness lists and retained experts. I've been gentlemanly about an awful lot in this litigation, but what you want is a great thing and you offer me nothing valuable in return. My bosses the tutors aren't going to let me squander this advantage.

You've known since November 1999 that I retained burn psychologist Dr. Carney. It is beyond me to understand why you did not take the opportunity in the last nine months to cultivate an opposing expert. Nor do I understand why you didn't hire one any time since the February pretrial order which clearly warned your client to retain experts prior to the August 1 witness list deadline. How have I possibly taken unfair advantage of you by sending you my expert's report two weeks before the deadline you ignored?

Do I owe you something because you hoped to see Dr. Carney's report before you hired your own expert? It's amazing to me that a seasoned litigator like you would blow a pretrial deadline. It's unseemly you'd whine about it. I think a prudent litigator would have started his expert on the 1,800 discovery pages a long time ago. I think a prudent litigator would have seen his expert's exam had to happen by September 1 and, observing my own struggle for a court order against DSS, obtain that permission or move for court order a long time ago.

I really don't understand why you are faulting me. Your right to retain an expert was nowhere conditioned upon my delivery of a report to you. On the other hand, your right to retain an expert and list him was deadlined at August 1. I supplied you with Dr. Carney's report the same day I received it, July 17. My delivery perfectly complied with C.C.P. art. 1465 and was well within the pretrial order's September 1 deadline.

So what am I supposed to say when you complain your medical discovery is not complete? "I feel sorry for you"? "I feel your pain" (not)? "There but for the grace of God" (maybe)? How about the aspirational Article IX of the LTLA Creed: "If a fellow member of the bar makes a **JUST** request for cooperation, or seeks scheduling accommodation, I will not **arbitrarily or unreasonably** withhold consent." Or, how about the pretrial order itself, "These cases will not be continued because counsel has not completed discovery."

You say all defense counsel agree it is "difficult, though not impossible" to mediate or prepare for trial on October 23. And your point is?

I don't see what advantage unrequited delay gives to Monique Meak. In fact, delay hurts her. Open you heart and listen to her reality. DSS is doing everything it can in order to free her for adoption. It is recruiting her mother's young cousin, a Texas social worker who earns 23K a year, to take Monique off DSS's hands. Problem is, Monique's needs are so huge that she'll either overwhelm this cousin or the cost of attendant services will bankrupt her, even after the meager DSS stipend. So do we take a shot and hope Monique's trust isn't harmed again and that she doesn't bounce back, or do we keep her in the institution until a kind, wealthy surrogate couple comes along? There is a third alternative: win Monique significant resources of her own. Her own money could help create a viable, permanent rescue. Naturally, such a plan will require judicial approval and oversight by persons independent of her caregiver. And, of course, CPS and Scottsdale will have no say in it.

The longer Monique is without resources of her own, the longer she is unable to affect her foster care and institutional status. Money is control is freedom. Do you understand now why I adamantly oppose any continuance? Why I'll fight to preserve her a trial free of witnesses other than those timely designated?

A delay isn't needed to get the mediation done. Pick a mutually convenient date, place and person and I'll sign a consent judgment requiring all of us to appear with authority and to work for a specified amount of time. DSS counsel said he's got someone in mind, in New Orleans, but no authority. I'll bring the tutors and we will happily participate, though I have grave reservations of success given how plaintiff's previous low offers met scoffing, hardened positions, and lack of authority. Now that I have pleaded the 1983 actions, cheap is gone.

So y'all want to know "how much you got in this case." Fuggeddabouddit. That's none of your client's damn business. I don't care how many times plaintiff's lawyers use this line on you. It's not what I do and it's not discoverable and it's not relevant. Think in terms of what the trier of fact is going to hear. How much has Monique been harmed, how much it is going to take to restore her, how much will end the threat of scalding in foster care?

I've got to hand it to you, Leonard, you are interesting. On one hand, in the phone call, you said that I was too close to my client, that I cared too much about what happened to her. That made me feel good and I think you wanted me to be flattered. I think you miss that good feeling in your own practice. Then, in your letter, you bitch to me that your inactivity has prejudiced your mediation position and thus I should join you to persuade Judge Gardner to reschedule the trial and give you a second chance to do what the long-noticed court order to you to do. Those two statements are inconsistent. How do you figure I should serve two masters? I can't keep Monique first AND 'give a hoot about CPS, too. Praise me then arm-twist me? It's chutzpah if you didn't realize your irrationality, manic depression if you can't help it, or jaded cynicism if you plan to exhibit your letter. Show yours and I'll show mine.

I absolutely plan to have Dr. Carney testify live at trial. The dates are reserved on her calendar. If it makes you feel better that Dr. Carney acknowledges Monique's preexisting conditions, so be it. Did you think I didn't know it too? I double-dare you to argue that Monique is less worthy because she was not a "perfect" child. Fact is, Monique's preexisting conditions are what makes her case compelling. It's why she was owed a heightened duty of care. And instead of slashing her damages, it's why we have is eggshell enhancement. Don't you remember the Sunday School lesson of the Widow's Mite? So what if Monique didn't start with plenty. What she lost -- no matter how little -- meant a lot to her.

It's astounding you wrote to ask if I had contacted Dr. Carney for available deposition dates. Did you dictate this before our three-way call to Galveston when we were given August 25 and 29, or are you forgetting things? Are your partners aware of this behavior, your clients? After we talked I put the dates to the other attorneys. Neither attorney for Allstate or the Whites returned my call before DSS counsel trashed both dates, saying he was on vacation on the 25th and didn't want to be bothered on the 29th, his first day back. I am taking no further responsibility to schedule Dr. Carney's deposition. I think I already know what she is going to say. If you want to notice her, I suggest that you clear dates before the September 1 discovery cut-off. I'll move anything except my other trials which are August 8th in the a.m., August 10th in the a.m., and my pre-paid, non-refundable legal seminar in Wyoming August 15th -22nd. I'll work at night or on a weekend. If you can't get two hours back to back, reserve two separate ones. Maybe we will finish in just one hour.

I strongly believe settlement is more likely if everyone could arrange for their principals to listen to Dr. Carney. If need be, I am willing to depose her after the cut-off. Just stay away from my other trials September 6th all day and September 12th in the a.m. That's the only untimely discovery I am consenting to.

About Monique displaying her scars: (1) she's not in my custody, and (2) the only display allowed is before a defense doctor or photographer. I expect you will confine yourself strictly to conduct permitted by the consent court order. As far as those "restrictions" you asked me to send, look at my letter dated June 25, 1998.

Last, you got Dr. Lyon's economic report the same day I did. You think those are big numbers? Want to settle instead for the present day value of Bethlehem's charge, $350 per day? You say you intend to use Dr. Boudreaux. Let me see his name on your date-stamped witness list, and a timely report, and maybe I'll stipulate to his numbers instead. No witness list? Then Boudreaux is toast.

Notice to all counsel: No one sent me a timely witness list. The deadline was August 1. Fax me your timely, date-stamped witness lists immediately, 822-0355. See C.C.P. art. 1313.

Notice to all counsel: Now I begin scheduling the pretrial attorney conference. Our time frame is October 13th through the 20th. I have NO conflicts in that time period. Each of you need to let me know what your available dates are. To make a good faith effort to mark and exchange exhibits, edit the depositions, craft admissibility and fact stipulations, jury charges and interrogatories, etc. is going to take a whole day. I don't think our judge is going to appreciate it if we say we hardly tried, or that little consensus was reached. Everyone is welcome to come to my home office to get this done, but I don't have a secretary. Let me know when you are available for a full day and if you have a location preference.

This letter caused all of the defense attorneys to prepare and send late witness lists, so Frazier filed a motion to strike containing this order:

IT IS ORDERED: that Barbara and Charles White, Allstate Insurance Company, Child Placement Services, Inc., Scottsdale Insurance Company, and the Louisiana Department of Social Services shall show cause on the 6th day of October, 2000 at 9:00 o'clock a.m. why all should not be declared in disobedience of the pretrial order for failure to file or for untimely filing of witness lists and, pursuant to C.C.P. arts. 1551(C) and 1471(2)-(4), why any just order should not be entered, including striking the untimely filed witness lists, prohibiting each defendant from calling witnesses at trial, and awarding plaintiff reasonable expenses and attorney's fees for this motion.

# CHAPTER 23

The Juvenile Court case met again on August 10th.
OCS said it is having problems getting Texas to certify the
cousin's home. An ASFA exception is not due for months.
Demetrius Jackson's surrender of parental rights fell through
because of a defect in service upon Lana Meak. Next status
hearing will occur on September 10th. Frazier was not pleased
to hear of the delay. He tried to keep in perspective that his
only client was Monique whereas the social workers were
busy with dozens of children. Nevertheless, Frazier decided to
vent his frustrations:

> Someone needs to prod Texas good and
> hard. There is no good reason for a home study
> to take this long. It is unnecessary that Monique
> should languish in a group home. She should be
> placed with her Texas cousin who, as a social
> work professional herself, is willing and able to
> care for the child.

> I haven't had an opportunity to talk with
> Miss Lisa Grande. I am cautiously optimistic we
> will rescue Monique from Bethlehem because
> Miss Grande read Dr. Carney's report and did not
> withdraw. Caring for Monique alone will be

daunting. My concern is that Monique does not boomerang from Grande. Monique's whole life has been crushed trust.

Monique has great needs. Dr. Carney outlined it best:

1. Placement in a stable family environment with care-taking assistance provided to the parent(s) of the family to prevent their exhaustion.

2. Family therapy/counseling provided by an expert.

3. Individual psychotherapy and psychiatric treatment for Monique with the goals of overcoming the effects of trauma and developing a positive body image and a positive self-regard.

4. A special education program that emphasizes socialization as well as academics and job training.

See July 17, 2000 report, last page. There will be a tremendous cost to supply these needs. See economist Dr. Marlon Lyon's report. Miss Grande isn't going to be able to pay for these services on her 23K salary. There is Monique's SSI check and Medicaid, but still there is a great shortfall.
Other financial support will be needed.

It's not enough to send Monique to Texas with just SSI and Medicaid and a $900/month stipend. What if Ms. Grande has to stop work in order to give Monique 24/7 one-on-one care.?

It's even worse if she keeps working because no subsidy will pay for replacement care services. I don't want to bounce Monique or bankrupt Ms. Grande.

Nor is the greater foster care stipend enough to cover Monique's great and unique needs. Nor is the post-adoption subsidy. More must be done.

It is DSS's problem to make up the shortfall, either by money or by delivering free services.

Obviously we want to keep her SSI and Medicaid eligible. For this reason, any tort recovery for the scalding will be tucked away in a special needs trust instead of merely held by DSS for lump sum distribution at adoption.

# CHAPTER 24

Skinner Auld finally managed to coordinate a date for Dr. Carney's deposition, August 29th. It will be by telephone conference call while Dr. Carney is videotaped. Frazier will go to Galveston while the other attorneys will be scattered across Louisiana.

Even before the deposition was taken there were Daubert grumblings. The defense attorneys were threatening to disqualify Dr. Carney. Essentially, a Daubert challenge means to protect the jury from receiving junk science by testing the expert's scientific method.

Frazier wrote to Dr. Carney to get her ready for the deposition and the Daubert attack.

> Your deposition will be taken by telephone on August 29th. Please have a current C.V. ready to fax to the defendants. I probably will not ask any questions at the deposition. If I need something from you, I'll let you know.
>
> The "boys" will not dwell on your education, work experiences, and publications before the middle 1980's. They will try to

denigrate your early work in hypnosis and in sexual therapy, but that will be just horsing around. Rather, the focus and high scrutiny will be on the reliability of your scientific method. Other experts may help prepare the questions. Expect that your published works, even conference papers, may be obtained and mined for inconsistent statements. You'll be asked for a list of leading books and articles so these might later be mined for inconsistent statements.

Expect probing into the scientific basis behind your opinions that there will be long term psychological effects, about the consequence of Monique's hidden scars, and about burn effects on the mentally disabled. Expect issues such as, if the field is relatively new and few burn victims have been studied for life, how reliable can long term opinions be? How can you reliably dissect, and predict, Monique's suffering when that suffering takes on aspects unique to her nurture (non-repeatable) and when nobody's studied a set of mentally challenged burn victims before (no basis for comparison)? How may a psychologist properly accept other provider's reports at face value, and rely on them, without personally knowing those providers or at least sampling the veracity of the information supplied? Doesn't that mean if you were supplied with bad information that your conclusions would be suspect?

Here is the crux of the exercise: how can you look at some photos, wade through a stack of papers from people you don't know, observe

Monique for two hours without her cooperation, and then opine catastrophe?

I strongly recommend reading <u>State v. Foret</u>, enclosed. This decision shows, in a psychology context, the factors used to test for reliable expert testimony. You may want to outline your thoughts on this.

The defense will also try to get you to embellish portions of your report on Monique. They may want an inventory of the documents I gave you, or your comment on a particular item. Feel free to refer to the serial numbers; everyone has the same set you have.

I hope you are looking forward to this opportunity to share your life's work and your passion. This won't be an Inquisition but there will be doubters and naysayers. Don't let them get under your skin. They are paid handsomely to tune out compassion.

Frazier flew back to Galveston the day before the deposition. He went to see Dr. Carney and they went over the expected questions. Then the videographer arrived and set up. Soon the phone rang. It was time to get started. The deposition lasted about an hour. As promised, Frazier asked no questions. Later, after Frazier returned home, he wrote Dr. Carney again:

> Thank you very much for the wonderful deposition. Unless the case sooner settles or the trial is moved, I'll be seeing you again in Galveston, for trial preparation, on <u>Wednesday October 18 from 2 p.m. until 5 p.m.</u>

> Mr. Auld believes he sprang a trap. He told me all about it. He says Monique deserves nothing for future losses. He figures the case is over because you candidly admitted most of your recommendations for Monique's future care were already needed before her burn.

> I think there is a disconnect somewhere. Yes, the first principle of personal injury law is one is only responsible for what one causes. But Mr. Auld would treat Monique like an old car. "Oh, that car was already beat up more than it would cost to fix. The last hit didn't do any recoverable damage."

> So, aside from the first 19 days of pain and suffering, and the body image therapy for the fading scar, does her burn even matter?

> I don't think Monique is a used car. I don't think you do, either. You refused to be baited into guessing "how much of today's Monique was due to the pre-existing condition, how much to the burn trauma, how much to the subsequent separation."

No one asked the obvious question: With all your experience, why can't you give us numbers for our model? I assume you would agree that the car model is flawed. A beaten pillow is a better metaphor.

Throughout life every human takes emotional blows of varied sources, various impacts. Sometimes full re-inflation occurs, given the right milieu, helpers and time. Sometimes the healing is halted by maladjustment due to some reason or another.

Imagine now this 4.5-year-old pillow called Monique has already taken several poundings -- born very premature to an underage mother, microencephalic, developmental delay, mildly mentally retarded, absentee father, neglected or abused by her mother -- surely she had not fully recovered from these poundings in just three months of foster care. This little pillow is punched in from all directions.

Now scald her. She didn't talk to you about the experience, but we know she sobbed because of the pain of the scald and the debridement. The psychological effect is unique to Monique because of her pre-existing traumas and disabilities. It merged with the pre-existing condition and made it more intractable. Think of a broken finger being crushed in a second accident.

What about the successive traumas and sex abuse allegations which occurred less than two years after the scald? Since Monique was not psychologically fully recovered from the burn, then the subsequent traumas affected her even more intensely. In other words, the pillow took another hit before it could re-inflate. The unhealed burn trauma made her more susceptible to psychological re-injury.

In the Juvenile Court on September 9th OCS announced that Monique had been freed for adoption by the formal voluntary surrenders of both parents. Frazier picnicked with Monique at Bethlehem. Two weeks later the Juvenile Court changed the plan of the case to adoption. OCS would make a trial placement of Monique with her cousin Miss Grande. In the meantime, she will stay at Bethlehem. At the end of that month, Frazier and his girls joined Monique and her friends on a Bethlehem outing to the Jazzland amusement park.

As the trial date grew closer, Frazier again wrote to Dr. Carney to prepare her for her trial testimony:

Here are copies of your deposition transcript and video. Please watch the video at least once before we meet on October 18th.

Turn the volume "off" and watch the non-verbal language. Be critical. Do you like this image? Is this lady open, candid, earnest? What would you change, if anything?

Next, try to imagine the trial. Play like you are waiting outside a darkly wooded, dimly lit small courtroom. No windows. The bailiff summons you. You walk up a narrow aisle into the pit, past the jurors and the lawyer. You stride up to the witness box, between the judge and the jury, step up, and settle in a heavy wooden chair. You are in a dark wood box. The lighting at the judge's bench, at the witness stand, and at the jury box is a bit better than elsewhere in the courtroom. There's a microphone in front of you but you can ignore it. Your voice will easily carry throughout the room.

You raise your right hand and take the witness oath. You can only communicate with your head, shoulders, arms and hands. Next to you is Judge Gardner. She is about your age. She is the mother of a handicapped child. She was one of the first women to break the glass ceiling at the court, and has been on the bench for about 15 years.

The jury box is on your other side. The 12 jurors are seated in two rows with a couple alternates nearby. The jurors come from every social level just like the parents at your hospital, but here they tend toward the female, minority, poor and less educated. It's OK to warmly look them over, face to face.

The lawyers are spread out below you. If I am not forced to stand at the lectern, then I will stand at the rail of the jury box so when you talk to me you will be talking to them. The other lawyers may stand in odd places in the courtroom in order to get you to turn away from the jurors. It's OK to address the jury whenever you speak.

You are there for Monique and for every burned child who has ever touched your heart. You'll have to be open and genuine in front of strangers for a couple of hours. It will go fast and it will be tiring. Imagine your dismount, and how the jurors acknowledge you as you go. You will do fine.

Next, Frazier booked an October 18th flight to meet and further prepare Dr. Carney in Galveston.

The mediation occurred October 3rd. All of the attorneys were there with authority to settle the case. The tutors were also present, having met with Frazier to devise a settlement strategy. When the mediation opened, all of the attorneys shared the good points of their positions, and knocked the bad points of the other parties' cases. The defense tried to brow-beat the tutors, telling them they ought to settle today rather than risk getting nothing at trial. Then the two sides broke apart into different rooms and the mediator shuttled back and forth between them.

When the mediator asked Frazier how much money it would take to settle the case, he said "One and a half million dollars." He and the tutors had planned this. The number was more than 10 times the offer from the last spring. The mediator was shocked. He asked why so high. Frazier answered, "Dr. Carney, Dr. Lyon, punitives, attorney's fees, and the jury venire."

The mediator left to relay Frazier's number to the defense attorneys. After a few minutes he returned, saying, "The defendants hardly agree about anything. They managed to pool their authority together and raise $125,000 to settle the case. This was your number last spring. Would you take it now?"

"Tell them the tutors and I believe $1.5 million is a conservative number for a very attractive plaintiff, a shocking and preventable injury, corporate and state defendants. and good experts. Remind them that the case has more than $250,000 in special damages," said Frazier. The mediator nodded and left again.

This time when he returned the mediator said the session was over because the defendants would not raise their offer, and the parties remained too far apart.

Three days later -- and three weeks before trial -- Frazier was back before Judge Gardner for a motions hearing and status conference. His motion to quash the defense witness lists was denied. The judge said the lists were technically untimely, but that plaintiff had not shown that he was prejudiced in any way. A little leeway should have been granted, said Judge Gardner.

Next, the attorney for the Whites made an oral motion to continue the October 23rd trial date, saying that he was involved in a political campaign and had no time to prepare for trial. Caught off guard, Frazier fought to keep the trial date, but to no avail. Judge Gardner granted the motion to continue the trial, and reset it five months away on March 26, 2001. All other pending motions were stayed. A new pre-trial order and cut-offs was issued.

Immediately after that hearing, the judge called all of the attorneys into chambers. The defendants complained about the failure of the mediation. Auld, taking the lead, said they had met the February demand of $125,000 but Frazier would not take it, that he now wanted a crazy number of $1.5 million. Auld said the plaintiff's case isn't worth that much because the child would not be in court and because his expert did not find future damages attributed to the scalding, if she wasn't knocked out on <u>Daubert</u> challenge. Judge Gardner said the case needed to be settled and must be settled and repeatedly questioned Frazier why the case was worth more than $125,000. Each point Frazier made (attractive plaintiff, horrible injury, high specials, good experts, possible punitive damages and attorney's fees) was met with scoffing denials by the defense attorneys. Judge Gardner's frown got deeper and deeper. She said she would be glad to hear a <u>Daubert</u> motion to knock out Dr. Carney, and may as well rule against plaintiffs on the civil rights exceptions.

Frazier was clearly pissing her off and, given her earlier performance that morning, he began to wonder if he was ever going to get a fair shake from Judge Gardner again. Further litigation in front of her promised time-killing writs and appeals. Finally, Frazier replied that he did not have authority to change the plaintiff's settlement offer. He had to take it up with the tutrix, and by coincidence she was available elsewhere in the building. Judge Gardner told Frazier to fetch the tutrix.

He found Alberta Jones in the Juvenile Court awaiting a case. Frazier told her about Judge Gardner's rulings and about her insistence on getting the case settled. He said fighting the judge was futile, and any trial would only mean lengthy appeals. It would be best to settle today. He suggested that

Jones counter-offer at $175,000 and take $150,000. Jones agreed.

Frazier returned to the status conference and relayed the counter-offer. The defense attorneys continued to balk, but this time Judge Gardner made some remarks about finding a middle ground. Auld groaned and said he thought he could raise $150,000. Frazier agreed to take it.

A few days later Frazier wrote this letter to DHH about its Medicaid lien.

> I told you today that plaintiff's tutrix and the defendants, on October 6, 2000, reached a verbal intent to settle for the in globo sum of $150,000.00.
>
> I asked you how much would DHH discount the medicals for my labor and costs. You said DHH would not discount the $17,114.61 at all because the net after the attorney's fees and costs is higher than the lien.
>
> Your interpretation of the law has not been litigated before. I wonder how much a negative precedent could affect your collection efforts. As long as you insist on no discount then we are headed to the judges.

I hereby notify all defense counsel that the settlement agreement will contain a provision stating plaintiff disputes the payment of $17,114.61 lien claimed by DHH, and that those disputed proceeds will remain escrowed in the registry of the court until a final judgment is had on the intervention.

Ms. Bordelon, you did none of the work. You did not even attend the mediation or the status conference.

Unlike Medicare, Medicaid's regulations are silent about reducing a lien because of the cost of recovery. As you know, where federal law is absent state law governs.

Under state law, the lien is extinguished by confusion, C.C. art. 1903. When the state has provided medical services to remedy its own tort, it has already partially satisfied its obligation to make the victim whole. This partial remedy is undone, and the plaintiff re-damaged, if the state can recoup medical costs from the sum it pays to settle the remainder of the state's liability. Whatever DSS pays is not money from a "third party."

Alternatively, under state law, a debt owed by subrogation is subject to reduction for the plaintiff's procurement costs. See R.S. 46:446(F), R.S. 9:4752, Mena v. Muhleisen Properties, 94-799 (La.App. 5 Cir. 2/15/95); 652 So.2d 65 and Barreca v. Cobb, 95-1651 (La. 2/28/96); 668 So.2d 1129.

At the least, Monique's tutrix is owed a 15% "friend of the court" incentive payment, 42 C.F.R. 433.153.

Two weeks later DHH offered a lien discount of 15%, which Frazier and the tutors accepted.

Frazier wrote to the witnesses and experts about the trial continuance. He also collected all of the unpaid bills and paid the Clerk of Court and Civil Sherriff their charges. He drafted settlement papers for the tutorship court and for Judge Gardner and circulated them among counsel. It took two months to wrap up the suit. Much paperwork in the tutorship action and even more in the civil action had to be edited and approved by all counsel. Tax forms were collected. When all of the documents were ready, Frazier arranged a signing at court. He faxed this letter to Judge Gardner and the defense attorneys:

I confirm a status conference at court at 8:30 a.m. on Wednesday, December 13, 2000.

I asked for this meeting to collect in one place everyone needed to sign for settlement, with their registry deposits, or to explore any problems with the court. The parties have worked since October 6th to perfect a written settlement for the lump sum of $150,000. The defendants split the price between themselves. We have an acceptable draft of the settlement forms (receipt and release, judgment, ancillary affidavits).

$145,000 has been raised and is ready for deposit to the registry. The remaining $5,000 is the Jackson's portion. The Jacksons offer a money judgment. The tutrix is reluctant to expose the minor's estate to collection risk. None of the other defendants is willing to pay the Jackson's share and take a money judgment from them. Some say the tutrix should not risk trial over $5,000.

DHH's Medicaid lien was reduced by 15% with the intervenor's consent. The tutrix desires the DSS to waive its foster care lien, R.S. 46:51.1. DSS ought not make its wards pay for their foster care with their own flesh, especially when DSS is an alleged tortfeasor and settlement contributor.

Last, DSS offered to draft the Special Needs Trust., but has no experience doing so. DSS would like an administrative role in the trust until Monique Meak leaves foster care. The tutrix believes settlement and deposit into the registry should not be held up when DSS can best address its trust concerns in the tutorship action before Judge Fredrickson.

Prior to the final settlement conference, Frazier met with the tutors to get their signatures on the settlement documents. Next, Frazier again saw Judge Fredrickson for his formal permission to settle the case. The judge was delighted to hear that Frazier had managed to get $150.000, a lien waiver and a lien reduction, for a $100,000 case. He approved the settlement and the use of a special needs trust.

Armed with approval from the tutorship court, Frazier was now ready to consummate the settlement. He met with all counsel and Judge Gardner for the signing and exchange of documents. The proceeds checks were deposited with the Clerk of Court and put into the court's registry. The consent judgment to dismiss, and the receipt and release, stated:

### CONSENT JUDGMENT TO DISMISS

On joint motion of counsel for plaintiff Alberta Jones as dative tutrix ad litem of the minor Monique Meak; counsel for defendant Allstate Insurance Co.; counsel for defendants

Child Placement Services, Inc. and Scottsdale Insurance Co.; counsel for defendant the Louisiana Department of Social Services, and counsel for the intervenor Department of Health and Hospitals;

IT IS ORDERED: All causes of action, claims for damages, and defenses asserted or capable of assertion herein between all parties, namely, plaintiff Alberta Jones as dative tutrix ad litem of the minor Monique Meak; defendants Allstate Insurance Co.; Child Placement Services, Inc. and Scottsdale Insurance Co.; the Louisiana Department of Social Services; and the intervenor Department of Health and Hospitals; as well as all other offices, agencies, departments, sections and division of the State of Louisiana, in addition to all employees, agents, officials and representatives of same; are hereby declared compromised without admission of liability, and dismissed with prejudice, each party to bear own costs, reserving to plaintiff all rights as to defendants Barbara White and Charles White individually.

IT IS FURTHER ORDERED: the terms of the parties' Release and Receipt are incorporated herein. All settlement funds shall name "Clerk of Court for the benefit of Monique Meak" as payee and shall be deposited into the Civil District Court registry.

IT IS FURTHER ORDERED: From the settlement funds the Clerk of Court shall pay $14,547.42 to the Department of Health and Hospitals (by mail to its attorney).

IT IS FURTHER ORDERED: All settlement funds not disbursed by this judgment shall be paid according to judgment rendered in the child's tutorship action, <u>In the Interest of</u> <u>M.M.</u>, C.D.C. No. 97-627 "E". The net proceeds accruing to Monique Meak shall be placed in a Special Needs Trust approved by the tutorship court.

IT IS FURTHER ORDERED: This compromise is declared to be in the best interests of the minor, Monique Meak.

<u>RELEASE AND RECEIPT</u>

STATE OF LOUISIANA

PARISH OF ORLEANS

BEFORE ME, the undersigned Notary Public, personally appeared Alberta Jones and Michael Harmon, the duly appointed dative tutrix and undertutor ad litem of the minor, Monique Meak (hereinafter referred to as "Appearers") who, being duly sworn in the presence of the undersigned witnesses, said or attested as follows:

1. Appearers acknowledge and understand these definitions:

a. Reserving all rights against Barbara White and Charles White, "Released Parties" means each of the persons and entities named below, none of whom admit liability but all of whom expressly deny all liability:

i) Allstate Insurance Co., Allstate Indemnity Co., and its agents, employees, servants, directors, executive officers, insureds, insurers, assigns, and all other persons, firms, partnerships or corporations liable or claimed to be liable.

ii) Child Placement Services, Inc., Scottsdale Insurance Company, and their agents, employees, officers, directors, attorneys and insurers.

iii) State of Louisiana through the Department of Social Services and intervenor Department of Health and Hospitals, as well as all other offices, agencies, departments, sections and divisions of the State of Louisiana, including all employees, agents, officials and representatives of same.

b. "Disputed Claims and Damages" means: any and all past, present and future losses, claims and demands, actions and causes of action, general damages for physical injuries and mental injuries, all special damages, loss of use, loss of service, wages, earnings, loss of earnings capacity, costs and expenses, court costs, attorney's fees and expenses, punitive damages, statutory damages, penalty statutes, claims for loss of consortium, wrongful death, survivors' actions, service, society, and/or loss of enjoyment of life, and compensation of any kind or nature whatsoever on account of or in any way growing out of personal injuries, property damages, medical expenses, breach of warranty, redhibition, and all other causes and rights of action and damages whatsoever, whether known or unknown to appearers, and resulting from an accident which occurred to Monique Meak on or about January 28, 1996 in the Parish of Orleans, State of Louisiana, and all causes and damages which were asserted or could have been asserted in the litigation titled, "Jones v. White," Civil District Court No. 97-628 "G".

2.   Appearers hereby release and forever discharge the "Released Parties" of and from any and all "disputed claims and damages" in consideration for payment by or on behalf of the "Released Parties" of $145,000.00 which has been deposited with the Clerk of Civil District

Court for the Parish of Orleans, State of Louisiana, said deposit evidenced by attached Exhibit "A".

3.   Appearers hereby acknowledge that this is a compromise of a doubtful and disputed claim, to which the "Released Parties" do not admit liability but expressly deny liability.

4.   As further cause, appearers accept the State of Louisiana, Department of Social Service's written assurance, attached as Exhibit "B", that the costs of Monique Meak's foster care will not be assessed against these settlement proceeds.

5.   As further cause, appearers accept from the intervenor, the State of Louisiana through the Department of Health and Hospitals, a full and final settlement and compromise of the Medicaid lien asserted the action, "Jones v.

White," Civil District Court No. 97-628 "G", for the sum of $14,547.42 payable from the settlement funds deposited in registry of the court, which lien settlement includes the Department of Health and Hospitals release of all parties to this action, all potential third parties, all insurers, all attorneys and law firms and tutors and trustees, from any other Medicaid or medical providers lien which was asserted or could have asserted in that litigation. Other than the lien released, the Department of Health and Hospitals reserves whatsoever residual rights, if any, which it may have in Monique Meak's anticipated Special Needs Trust after her death.

6. Appearers acknowledge that Monique Meak's injuries may be permanent and progressive, and recovery from the injuries is uncertain and indefinite, and, in making this

release and agreement, appearers rely wholly upon their own judgment, belief and knowledge of the nature, extent and duration of the injuries, and appearers have not been influenced to execute this release by any representation or statement made by any released party, or by any released party's representative or any health care professional employed by any released party, regarding the injuries or any other matters whatsoever.

7. The "Released Parties" are hereby released from all claims and actions asserted against them in the matter, "Jones v. White," Civil District Court No. 97-628 "G", on the docket of the Civil District Court, Parish of Orleans, State of Louisiana, and appearers hereby direct their attorney of record in said action to

dismiss the suit, with prejudice, and with each party to bear his own cost.

8.    Except to enforce this settlement agreement, appearers agree that Monique Meak, her tutors and trustees, will not engage in further litigation or execute any judgment which would expose the released parties to any liability for the January 28, 1996 accident.

9.    Appearers have no knowledge whether any portion of Monique Meak's claim has been assigned, subrogated, transferred, liened or privileged, except for the items described in plaintiff's counsel's attached affidavit. Appearers intend to disclose and pay, with tutorship court approval, those items not paid by the dismissal of the tort action. Appearers have not entered into any contract of employment with any attorney other than the undersigned attorney.

10. This release agreement contains all terms and conditions of the settlement agreement between appearers and the "Released Parties." The terms of this release agreement are contractual and not a mere recital. Appearers have carefully read this release agreement; they understand its contents, and they sign it as free agents for the purposes herein set forth.

By getting DSS and court approval to hire outside counsel to supply a special needs trust. Frazier consciously broke the law, C.C.P. art. 683. That law requires the net proceeds from a foster child's lawsuit be kept by DSS in a spendthrift trust until the child reaches age 18 or leaves foster care. Had Frazier followed the law, Monique would get a large lump sum on the day of her adoption, which money would have disqualified her for SSI and Medicaid until spent. To prevent such a disaster, Foster put Monique's money into a special needs trust which would go with her when adopted. The trust specified that Frazier, the original trustee, could transfer the trusteeship to the adoptive parent, which was expected to be Miss Grande of Texas. Copies of the trust were filed in court and given to DSS and DHH.

Next, Frazier returned to Judge Fredrickson in the tutorship court with a motion and order to disburse the funds in the registry. That pleading stated:

## MOTION TO DISBURSE

Now comes Alberta Jones tutrix ad litem for Monique Meak who, with the consent of the undertutor ad litem, Michael Harmon, moves for orders to disburse the Jones v. White, CDC No. 97-628 "G" settlement proceeds held in the registry of the court.

1.

Mover approves this settlement statement:

INCOME
Louisiana Department of Social Services                $92,500.00

| | |
|---|---|
| Scottsdale Insurance Company | 42,500.00 |
| Allstate Insurance Company | 10,000.00 |
| | $145,000.00 |

FEES AND EXPENSES

| | |
|---|---|
| Thomas Frazier attorney's fee | $48,333.33 |
| Thomas Frazier invoiced expenses | 19,785.10 |

TO BE PAID

| | |
|---|---|
| Forensic Economic Corp., expert | 1,450.00 |
| Dr. Wanda Carney, expert | 700.00 |
| Atty. Carole Smathers, SNT | 1,112.50 |
| Atty. Alberta Jones, tutrix | 2,615.00 |
| Atty. Michael Harmon, undertutor | 500.00 |

MEDICAID LIEN

| | |
|---|---|
| Dept. of Health and Hospitals | 14,547.42 |
| | $89,043.35 |

NET

| | |
|---|---|
| Monique Meak Special Needs Trust | $55,956.65 |

SUMMARY

| | |
|---|---|
| Litigation (51%) | $74,495.93 |
| Medicaid Lien (10%) | 14,547.42 |
| Trust Proceeds (39%) | 55,956.65 |
| | $145,000.00 |

INVOICED EXPENSES

| | |
|---|---|
| $4,227.50 | attorneys (Smathers, Jones, Harmon) |
| 1,855.80 | copies |
| 1,420.12 | court costs, Civil Sheriff and Clerk of Court |
| 3,200.00 | depositions |

| | |
|---:|:---|
| 3,900.00 | experts |
| 1,738.10 | investigation, exhibits and research |
| 187.51 | long distance |
| 213.65 | meetings |
| 201.67 | mileage, parking, cab fare, air fare |
| 592.28 | photography |
| <u>432.47</u> | postage |
| $19,785.10 | TOTAL |

2.

Upon the disbursement, attorney Thomas Frazier shall pay the listed third parties.

3.

In support, mover attaches:

Exhibit 1: Consent Judgment to Dismiss, <u>Jones v. White,</u> CDC No. 97-628 "G".

Exhibit 2: contract and invoices, attorney Thomas Frazier.

Exhibit 3: statements from Forensic Economic Corporation, Dr. Wanda Carney, Carole Smathers, and Alberta Jones.

Exhibit 4: original, "Monique Meak Special Needs Trust"

Exhibit 5: White bankruptcy correspondence.

### 4.

This tutorship shall continue (1) to oversee the trustee's management, and (2) to pursue the claim against the Whites.

### 5.

Movers believe this disbursal is in the best interests of the child, Monique Meak. Movers pray the disbursement be ordered.

## CLERK'S CERTIFICATE OF FUNDS

On December 13, 2000, the registry received $145,000.00 in the action Jones v. White, CDC No. 97-628 "G". The order directed payment of $14,547.42 to the Department of Health and Hospitals. The remaining funds,

$130,452.58, are collected and available for disbursement.

## ORDER

Considering the motion, exhibits and consents,

IT IS ORDERED: the Clerk of Court shall disburse SEVENTY-FOUR THOUSAND FOUR HUNDRED NINETY-FIVE AND 93/100 ($74,495.93) DOLLARS payable to Thomas Frazier, who shall in turn pay the third parties listed in the motion.

IT IS FURTHER ORDERED: the Clerk of Court shall disburse the sum of FIFTY-FIVE THOUSAND NINE HUNDRED FIFTY-SIX AND 65/100 ($55,956.65) DOLLARS to "Monique Meak Special Needs Trust by its trustee, Thomas Frazier", who shall maintain these funds in a federally insured deposit account within the terms of the trust instrument. The "Monique Meak Special Needs Trust:" instrument is approved in the best interests of the child, Monique Meak. Mr. Frazier shall direct the trust's financial depository to send duplicate monthly statements to the tutrix, Alberta Jones.

IT IS FURTHER ORDERED: the Clerk of Court shall disburse to "Monique Meak Special Needs Trust by its trustee, Thomas Frazier" whatsoever interest as may have accrued upon all sums on deposit.

IT IS FURTHER ORDERED: The tutrix is authorized to settle the claim against Barbara White and Charles White for $5,000 from their bankruptcy trustee or any other tribunal with jurisdiction over the claim.

# CHAPTER 25

Frazier pursued the Whites into the bankruptcy court by filing this Proof of Claim in their Chapter 13 case.

Now by undersigned counsel comes creditor Alberta Jones, in her capacity as the dative tutrix ad litem of the minor Monique Meak, to submit proof of an unsecured claim for $5,000. The creditor reserves the right to supplement this Proof of Claim with other documents from the voluminous four-year state court litigation.

| | | |
|---|---|---|
| 1. | Photo | Monique Meak with scalding scar |
| 2. | 02/15/96 Children's | Discharge Summary |
| 3. | 02/19/96 Children's | Child Abuse Consultation |
| 4. | 01/28/97 Tort | Petition |
| 5. | 03/17/97 Tutorship | Tutrix Appointment |
| 6. | 06/02/97 Tort | First Supp. & Amended Petition |
| 7. | 10/04/99 Tort | Second Supp. & Amended Petition |
| 8. | 07/10/00 Dr. Carney | Expert Report |
| 9. | 12/04/00 Tutorship | Authority to Settle with Whites |
| 10. | 12/12/00 Tort | Release and Receipt |
| 11. | 12/13/00 Tort | Dismissal |
| 12. | 12/28/00 Tutorship | Authority to Settle with Whites |

Frazier appeared at the Meeting of Creditors where the trustee confirmed the debt with the Whites. Thereafter, Frazier received an installment check every month for about three years until the full $5,000 was paid. From each check he deducted his attorney's fee, and deposited the rest into the trust.

# CHAPTER 26

Monique spent the Christmas 2000 holidays with Lisa Grande in Texas. However, she came back early to Bethlehem. It was suspected that Monique embarrassed her Texas family by being incontinent at a wedding, or that she was starting to resume her hyperactive-aggressive ways. In fact, the early return was a quirk in her ticketing and had nothing to do with her behavior. She was scheduled to visit Texas again in the spring, and would probably be placed there in May with an adoption in November or December 2000.

Bethlehem made a medicine change on the hunch that the Ritalin had stopped working, or because her condition was getting worse with the onset of puberty hormones.

Frazier and two of his daughters visited Monique at Bethlehem on January 13th. They brought Christmas gifts and lunch from McDonald's. They talked about her Christmas trip to Texas and her hopes for the future.

OCS's February 19, 2001 court letter reported that Monique was disciplined for committing oral sex on a boy on a school bus.

In April she flew to Texas for an Easter visit with Ms. Grande. However, when summer 2001 arrived, Monique was still at Bethlehem. OCS said it was having trouble getting paperwork from the Texas social workers. Missing were proofs that training classes had been completed, and a home study.

Monique flunked special education and she didn't pass the LEAP exam. Her score was too low to expect that she could pull it up. OCS decided against sending her to summer remediation classes because her failure to learn was caused by her mental retardation. Her next IEP will start her in special education all over again. It didn't help, too, that Monique was a disciplinary problem. All year long the school tried to expel her due to her bad conduct and fighting.

Fed up with the inactivity, in July Frazier filed a motion to inspect agency records:

> Monique Meak and her attorney wonder why she hasn't moved to Texas yet. Chats with the social worker and BGC haven't gotten to the root of the problem. Due to a lack of specific knowledge of what is broken, child's counsel hasn't been able to diagnose a fix. More knowledge is needed. Monique Meak moves to inspect and copy the department's case records, Ch.C. art. 652(A)(3).

By August OCS had straightened out. Monique was sent to Texas for a 30-day visit and that visit was expected to extend permanently when OCS converted the case to relative placement.

Frazier wrote to Ms. Grande:

Thank you for speaking recently with Mrs. Alberta Jones, Monique's tutrix, who relayed your concerns to me. Some were forwarded to OCS for action (enclosed).

I was glad to hear that you've coped well with Monique's ups and downs. I think she'll be calmer when she's certain that she is in a loving place and won't be going anywhere. Mrs. Jones was very impressed with you, and she's a tough critic. I'm glad Monique is with you.

Mrs. Jones said you did not have an attorney for the adoption. In that case, I can share the following information directly with you.

Monique does have a special needs trust fund. It's her money from a lawsuit for being scalded on the right leg and buttocks in a foster home. Mrs. Jones said you didn't know if you wanted control of the money or not. The way I had the papers written, I am the trustee but I can transfer the trusteeship to whoever adopts Monique. It's really up to you. If you take it, you'll have to keep the account records, file annual tax returns, and make sure the money is spent only in ways that do not disqualify Monique for SSI and Medicaid (that's the whole purpose of the SNT – so Monique won't lose her entitlements, but can have the benefit of her money, too.) Should she die, the money will belong to her estate.

So far, Mrs. Jones and I have not seen reason to use any of the SNT funds. The account has been earning interest and growing with periodic payments from the former foster parents (they ran into Bankruptcy Court and I followed them there to get Monique's money).

The only expected disbursement this year will be in December when Mrs. Jones and I will draw our administration fees. These expenses should be paid then in order to reduce the year 2001 taxes. I will prepare that tax return in the Spring of 2002.

If you adopt around February and become the trustee, you will have a full year before needing to file the next trust tax return. You can hire an accountant to do it for you. It is expected that you will not take a fee for your services to the trust but, if you do, those fees will be taxable income to you.

The trickiest thing is not spending the SNT funds on inappropriate items, and not accumulating countable assets which would cause Monique to lose her SSI and Medicaid. The SNT funds are not to be used for necessities like food, clothing and rent since it is presumed the entitlements cover these. However, SNT funds can be used for other things not provided by government. It is especially appropriate to use the money to meet Monique's special needs, for example tutoring or burn survivor camp. But the funds can be used more broadly, e.g. piano lessons, a bike, a car and insurance when she is licensed, or even a vacation (including one adult escort).   Be careful about buying non-consumables (e.g. fancy clothes or jewelry or other personal property) because, if their total value exceeds $2,000, then SSI and Medicaid will be lost.

You've got plenty of time to decide if you want to become trustee of the SNT.   In the meantime, if there is some unmet need, or some reasonably priced service, you'd like to get for Monique with her money, let me know.   Mrs. Jones and I are convinced you have Monique's best interests at heart, so we will be receptive to your request.

On another subject:   I've asked to participate in the adoption subsidy negotiations to try to get the best package of assistance available. The more coming in your home, the easier it will be for you to care for Monique.

I encourage you to begin asking Texas Social Services to supply you with an adoption attorney.   There are several important issues which must be worked out before the adoption takes place, including where the adoption occurs, the terms of the adoption subsidy, and which state will pay it. These issues can take some time to solve.   You should obtain professional help. Your attorney could probably use these items:

1. an informational page from Faces of Adoption web site;
2. Louisiana Revised Statutes 46:1790-1794, and

3. Louisiana Administrative Code 67:V.4901-4903.

Frazier learned that Monique had not enrolled in school in Texas because OCS failed to send her immunization record. Bethlehem said they faxed it to OCS, and said that Monique's shots needed updating. Within two weeks Monique received 13 shots so she could start school. Bethlehem was told to ship Monique's things to Texas. However, before August ended, Monique was sent back to Bethlehem because the Texas social workers failed to perform a home study before her 30 day visit expired. Relative placement, and adoption, were being held up because professionals were not doing their jobs.

In September 2001 Frazier again visited Monique at Bethlehem. She said she likes seeing Ms. Grande in Texas, and she is eager to return. Arrangements were made to ship her back to Texas around Thanksgiving. In fact, the Texas social workers got a move on because the paperwork was completed by Halloween. Yet, on November 18th, Frazier was still able to visit her at Bethlehem. She was still eager to be with Ms. Grande. For unknown reasons, another four months would pass before Monique went back to Texas.

The adoption was expected to occur in Summer 2002. A new IEP kept Monique from being promoted to middle school. She would be held back and given remedial instruction. Basically, the school would try to teach 10-year-old Monique how to complete kindergarten and get promoted to first grade. Her cognitive problems stemmed from her birth disabilities.

Frazier filed tax returns for the trust. In April, Frazier prepared and filed a motion to modify the disposition. That motion said:

> Nowhere in a State court letter will you find the true story of how the agency, despite orders to meet ALL the child's needs, tells foster parents that there is no money for some need or another.
>
> Not wants. NEEDS.

Like after-school daycare for single parent Lisa Grande, who's been footing a $64 per week care bill the State refuses to pay, ever since Monique was placed last November. Why? The big lie. *There is no money,* says DSS. Meet all needs of the child, says the court orders.

Or, how about the twice-per-week tutoring specially ordered because 10-year-old Monique isn't functioning at a first grade level? Lisa Grande engaged a tutor to make home visits at $100 per week, then is forced to discontinue because DSS will not fully reimburse her, notwithstanding court order.

Amicable demand was made, with legal references, but no reply. An affidavit with documentary evidence from Lisa Grande will be submitted.

Monique Meak seeks (1) an order specifically describing that DSS is obligated to fund her daycare and tutoring, at current levels and should those levels increase in the summer if she is not taken into Extended School Year; (2) an order particularly identifying the individuals responsible for those future payments to occur in a timely manner; and (3) a judgment in favor of Lisa Grande and against DSS to reimburse her for benefits withheld, and to fund Monique Meak for additional tutoring time for the sessions missed, legal interest from date of judgment.

OCS replied that it was already giving Ms. Grande the maximum in support and that it was barred from giving her a dime more. Frazier sent $520.00 from the trust to help Ms. Grande with the daycare and tutoring expenses. When she asked for $3,405 so Monique could attend a special needs summer camp, and sent the camp brochure, Frazier with tutrix approval dipped into the trust and sent the money to her along with an extra $300 for gear and clothes. Monique did go to the camp, but got kicked out for fighting.

By August 2002 Ms. Grande had an adoption attorney. Frazier wrote him:

> You represent Ms. Lisa George, adopting parent of Monique Meak. I am the trustee of the Monique Meak Special Needs Trust. The trust consists solely of a savings account valued at approximately $52,377.04.
>
> The trust instrument that permits me to transfer control of the trust to Monique's adoptive parent. I want to do this at the same time Ms. George comes from Texas to New Orleans for the adoption.
>
> Attached is the notice I need to file with the Internal Revenue Service in order to put Ms. George in charge. Before the hearing, please give me:
> (1) the adoption hearing date,
> (2) Ms. George's social security number.
>
> I must collect Ms. George's signature and a certified copy of the adoption judgment.

Also in August, Frazier paid Ms. Grande $900 to take Monique on a vacation to California.

Monique was finally adopted by Ms. Grande in March 2003. She requested an entire copy of Monique's cases, both the scalding case and Juvenile Court, and an accounting of all funds. These copies were made, along with the accounting, and were sent to her. Also sent was an IRS document transferring the trusteeship to Ms. Grande. Frazier prepared his final tax returns for the trust and found no taxes due.

Ms. Grande had questions about attorney fees and they were answered to her satisfaction. She signed and returned the IRS document. When Frazier received it, and certified proof of the adoption, he sent the trust funds to her. Over the next year or so, Frazier sent to Ms. Grande 2/3 of any check that trickled in from the White bankruptcy. When the $5,000 was finally paid, Frazier prepared a motion to withdraw from the Juvenile Court case, citing the adoption. He prepared a final accounting of the trust. He also filed a motion to terminate the tutorship:

<u>MOTION TO TERMINATE TUTORSHIP</u>

The motion of dative tutrix Alberta Jones and dative undertutor Michael Harmon:

1.

On January 28, 1996 the minor Monique Meak was scalded in a foster home in Orleans Parish.

2.

The minor's tutors commenced a tort action on Monique Meak's behalf, Jones v. White, CDC No. 97-628 "G", which concluded favorably. Judicial approval was obtained to create a special needs trust to receive the net proceeds, C.C.P. art. 4269.1. The original trustee of the Monique Meak Special Needs Trust was Thomas Frazier, counsel below.

3.

This tutorship should be terminated due to loss of jurisdiction.

## 4.

Monique Meak no longer lives in Louisiana. She is domiciled in the State of Texas with Ms. Lisa Grande, her adoptive mother. See adoption judgment of the Orleans Parish Juvenile Court. Thus, jurisdiction is ended, C.C.P. art. 4031.

## 5.

Monique Meak has no property in this State. The Special Needs Trust is a separate legal entity. A final accounting is attached. The new trustee is the adoptive mother in Texas. Thus, no jurisdiction lies under C.C.P. art. 4032.

## 6.

WHEREFORE, because Monique Meak is domiciled out of state and has no property in this state, then this Court no longer has tutorship jurisdiction, C.C.P. art. 4031-4032. This tutorship should be terminated, the final accounting should be accepted, and the tutors should be removed from their offices.

## CONSENT

We have reviewed this motion and the attached exhibits, and we consent to the prayer without any reservation.

## JUDGMENT

Considering the motion to terminate the tutorship, the attached exhibits, and C.C.P. art. 4031-4032,

IT IS ORDERED that this tutorship is terminated; the final accounting is accepted, and dative tutrix Alberta Jones and dative undertutor Michael Harmon are removed from their offices.

# CHAPTER 27

A long time after it was all over, Frazier confided in a letter to the tutrix:

> I was going over some old records and discovered that I spent about 962 hours working on Monique's scalding case. That means I earned about $50 per hour. I'm not 100% happy the case settled. I would have loved an award of attorney's fees.
>
> What I regret the most is, could I have done more to prove the psychological effects of the scalding, and to explain its synergy with her pre-existing conditions? Monique's failure to open up with Dr. Carney really hurt the case. It made Dr. Carney ripe for a <u>Daubert</u> strike, because opinions based only on the treatment of thousands are educated guesses at best and speculative at worst. The law doesn't fit mentally retarded children. If a tree falls in the forest and the only person there is a deaf mute, did the tree really fall?
>
> I'm most proud about listening to Skinner Auld complain that I had lost my objectivity, that it had gotten personal, that I cared for my client too much. He wasn't happy that my §1983 civil rights amendment forced him to plead that his client was merely negligent.
>
> I'm also proud that Monique's suit brought lasting changes to the foster care system. Now

foster homes are actually inspected instead only checking a list while sitting on the couch. And all foster homes are now required to have automatic anti-scald devices installed at the water heater. The state pays to have the work done because it is cheaper to prevent another Monique.

My daughters and I miss visiting Monique. I lost contact with her after her adoption.

Ms. Grande once told me she was going to invest Monique's money in rental real estate to get Monique an income stream. Whether she actually did this or not, I don't know. I hope she has not had any trouble with SSI or Medicaid.

I did find out that Monique is still getting into trouble. An Internet search revealed that she, at age 18, got arrested for pulling down a rack of candy in a convenience store. Monique was arrested again at age 21 for simple battery. Her booking photo plainly shows her small head and googly eyes.

If you liked this book, tell a friend. Put a post on Facebook, and review it at Amazon.com. Thank you.

briancad@yahoo.com

www.ingramcontent.com/pod-product-compliance
Lightning Source LLC
Chambersburg PA
CBHW051307220526
45468CB00004B/1239